FROM LEMONS
TO LEMONADE

FROM LEMONS TO LEMONADE

SQUEEZE EVERY LAST DROP OF SUCCESS OUT OF YOUR MISTAKES

Dean A. Shepherd

Vice President, Publisher: Tim Moore
Associate Publisher and Director of Marketing: Amy Neidlinger
Wharton Editor: Steve Kobrin
Acquisitions Editor: Jennifer Simon
Editorial Assistant: Pamela Boland
Development Editor: Russ Hall
Operations Manager: Gina Kanouse
Digital Marketing Manager: Julie Phifer
Publicity Manager: Laura Czaja
Assistant Marketing Manager: Megan Colvin
Cover Designer: Alan Clements
Managing Editor: Kristy Hart
Project Editor: Anne Goebel
Copy Editor: Gayle Johnson
Proofreader: Leslie Joseph
Indexer: Lisa Stumpf
Compositor: Bumpy Design
Manufacturing Buyer: Dan Uhrig

Wharton School Publishing offers excellent discounts on this book when ordered in quantity for bulk purchases or special sales. For more information, please contact U.S. Corporate and Government Sales, 1-800-382-3419, corpsales@pearsontech-group.com. For sales outside the U.S., please contact International Sales at international@pearson.com.

Printed in the United States of America

First Printing April 2009

ISBN-10 0-13-136273-9
ISBN-13 978-0-13-136273-4

Pearson Education LTD.
Pearson Education Australia PTY, Limited.
Pearson Education Singapore, Pte. Ltd.
Pearson Education North Asia, Ltd.
Pearson Education Canada, Ltd.
Pearson Educación de Mexico, S.A. de C.V.
Pearson Education—Japan
Pearson Education Malaysia, Pte. Ltd.

Library of Congress Cataloging-in-Publication Data

Shepherd, Dean A.

  From lemons to lemonade : squeeze every last drop of success out of your mistakes / Dean A. Shepherd.

    p. cm.

  Includes bibliographical references.

  ISBN 0-13-136273-9 (hbk. : alk. paper) 1. Success in business—Psychological aspects. 2. Business failures—Psychological aspects. 3. Failure (Psychology) I. Title.

  HF5386.S4277 2009

  650.1—dc22

                        2008041534

THIS BOOK IS DEDICATED TO
MY DAUGHTER, MEG,
FOR THE REASONS STATED
IN THE BOOK'S CONCLUSION.

CONTENTS

ACKNOWLEDGMENTS

The inspiration for writing this book are my father and mother, who experienced a great loss when our family business failed. They showed great courage, honor, and determination to "pull themselves up by the boot laces." These attributes are reflected in my brother, Brent, and sister, Kerrie, and I wanted to acknowledge them as part of the book's underlying story. My wife, Suzie, and my children, Jack and Meg, are a source of personal learning. They feel no reluctance in pointing out my failures. I also appreciate the contributions from my good mates, Professors Johan Wiklund, Mike Haynie, Melissa Cardon, Jeff Covin, and Don Kuratko, who have been instrumental in helping develop my ideas on this topic, which has led to the publication of a number of research articles. Finally, I would like to thank Jennifer Simon and Steve Kobrin for their vision and optimism with this project, and Russ Hall and Amanda Moran for their invaluable help.

ABOUT THE AUTHOR

Dean Shepherd is the Randall L. Tobias Chair in Entrepreneurial Leadership and Professor of Entrepreneurship at the Kelley School of Business, Indiana University. Professor Shepherd received his doctorate and MBA from Bond University (Australia) and a bachelor of applied science from the Royal Melbourne Institute of Technology. His research is in the field of entrepreneurial leadership. He investigates the decision making involved in leveraging cognitive and other resources to act on entrepreneurial opportunities. He also investigates the processes of learning from experimentation and failure, in ways that ultimately lead to high levels of individual and organizational performance. Professor Shepherd's research has been published in the top management and entrepreneurship journals. He has also authored or edited eight research books on entrepreneurship and strategy. His coauthored entrepreneurship textbook (with Hisrich and Peters) is in its seventh edition. He is an associate editor for the *Journal of Business Venturing*. He also is on the review board for numerous journals and is a panelist for the National Science Foundation (Innovation and Organization Science).

"THERE ARE NO SECRETS TO SUCCESS.
IT IS THE RESULT OF PREPARATION, HARD
WORK, AND LEARNING FROM FAILURE."
—COLIN POWELL

"EVEN HIS GRIEFS ARE A JOY LONG
AFTER TO ONE THAT REMEMBERS ALL
THAT HE WROUGHT AND ENDURED."
—HOMER

CHAPTER 1

MANAGING EMOTIONS TO LEARN FROM FAILURE

I once had a painful experience from which I learned a great deal, and it motivated me to share with you the insight I gained. If you are a normal person, you will have obstacles, setbacks, and outright failures. For some people these sting

If you are a normal person, you will have obstacles, setbacks, and outright failures.

like the dickens; for others they lead to total collapse. Part of what I want to help you with is how to be better prepared not only to expect to deal with some failure, but to be better able to deal with it when it comes, and to actually derive some good from it. But this is not as easy as just saying it, as I was to find out myself.

I had always taught my management students not to be discouraged by failure, that we learn more from our failures than our successes. I had even said that failure is often the fire that tempers the steel of one's learning and street savvy. Then I got the opportunity to test the wisdom of those words myself when I received a phone call from my father about twelve years ago. He told me that the family business that he had created twenty-odd years ago was in trouble. When I found out how much trouble, I told him he needed to notify creditors and close the business immediately. The business was closed, and due to director's guarantees to creditors, he lost his personal wealth.

My father exhibited a number of worrying emotions. There were numbness and disbelief that this business he created and managed for all those years was gone. There was some anger toward the economy, competitors, and creditors. Stronger emotions than anger were guilt and self-blame. He felt guilty that he had caused the failure of the business; guilty that the business could no longer be passed on to my brother; and guilty that not only had he failed as a businessman, but felt that he had failed as a father. This caused him great distress and anxiety. He felt the situation was hopeless, and he became withdrawn and at times depressed. His emotional state caused the rest of the family great distress and anxiety.

Because the business was an important part of my father, he found it difficult to separate himself from its failure. The business failure was not an event divorced from his personal identity. It was a deeply emotional event. Yet over time he was able to recover, and eventually he personally grew as a result of the experience. The failure event had provided a trigger to a regenerative and growth process. However, not all people recover and personally grow from failure.

Whether from thinking about my father, or about the ability of those who fail to grow from the experience, I realized that I could not accept the implicit assumption that learning from failure is automatic and instantaneous.

Learning from failure is not instantaneous; it requires time.

Learning from failure is not instantaneous; it requires time. It is not automatic; it requires a process that can be managed such that learning from failure can be maximized. Failure is an event that can touch us deeply and, in doing so, it presents some challenges. If these challenges can be overcome, failure presents the opportunity to personally grow from the experience.

By recognizing that failure can trigger a negative emotional reaction, we realize that learning from failure requires time. It also requires a process of dealing with the emotions generated by failure to learn from the experience. That process, once learned, can become one of your strengths instead of a weakness. It can be a very positive force in your life.

This can work one way or the other for you. It depends on how well you absorb the lesson. Take the comparative stories of Judy and Andrew. Judy had long dreamed of becoming a partner at a prestigious advertising agency. She had taken her first steps toward achieving this dream. She had recently completed her MBA (focusing on marketing) and had accepted a job at her preferred agency in New York City. The agency had an "up or out," "churn" human resources policy. That is, the agency hired many "juniors" and set high standards so that only the best and brightest would survive and be promoted. Judy needed to land six new major accounts in her first three years.

After weeks of cold calling, she finally secured her first meeting with a potential client. Judy had three weeks to prepare her marketing plan and pitch for the company's new, revolutionary product. Judy poured her heart and soul into the marketing plan and perfecting her pitch. She drew on her experiences with developing and delivering marketing plans as part of her MBA and her internships over the past two summers, and she diligently followed the "textbook" approach. However, her pitch was a failure, and she lost the account. The executives of the target company told her that her presentation reflected a lack of knowledge of their product and their company; that the theme across the marketing mix was, at best, ambiguous; and that it did not articulate the unique selling proposition. Judy's boss was particularly displeased, because his biggest rival picked up the account.

Judy was shattered. That pitch had represented her best effort. It had been a part of her life 24 hours a day, seven days a week, for three weeks. She felt embarrassed and depressed. As she again recalled the executives' comments, she was angry that they had missed the major points of her presentation and was disappointed in her boss for being persuaded by such uncreative "business types."

A few weeks later, Judy's friend Andrew also had a pitch rejected. He also felt bad, even though he knew that across his firm only one in five pitches landed an account.

Weeks after the pitch failure, Judy reviewed the comments offered by the executives and her boss. When she received her next chance, she made changes to avoid the sort of confusion she had created last time. She followed her boss's recommendations to focus the presentation and plan on only three key, distinctive points and to leave ample time for questions and answers at the end to address any unresolved issues. She now had a better idea of how to highlight the distinctive attributes of the potential client's product and to position it within the company's reputation in the marketplace, relative to its other products, and relative to competitors' products. She landed the client. She continued to improve from her mistakes, and by the end of her first year she had landed three additional accounts.

In contrast, Judy's friend Andrew blamed his rejection on the potential client's incompetence, and he disregarded that company's comments and those from his boss. He used the same approach (that had been so successful in school and unsuccessful in the "real world") with the next client. It failed again, and he lost the account. He repeatedly ignored comments about why his pitch was rejected. Andrew became even more frustrated and depressed. He came to believe that his dream of being an ad executive outmatched his ability to succeed at this career. He quit and went back to work in the family firm.

Judy and Andrew both had a negative emotional reaction to their projects being rejected. But Judy was able to manage that reaction and learn, and thus, increase her likelihood of success with subsequent pitches. Andrew did not learn. He made the same mistakes and continued to fail. Andrew knew the old saying that we can learn more from our failures than our successes, but he was unable to do so.

As you can see, project failure can lead to one of three possible outcomes:

- The emotional pain is so great for the person experiencing failure that he gives up and does not try again.

- The person responsible for the failure blames others and not himself and throws himself into the next project. He has not learned the reasons for the project's failure and is destined to make the same mistakes repeatedly.

- The person manages the emotions generated by the project failure so that they are less painful, occur for a shorter period, and no longer keep her from learning from that failure.

In this book, I focus on providing strategies and techniques to help you avoid the first two outcomes in order to achieve the third.

❁

Learning from Failure Is Difficult but Rewarding

Our projects typically are important to us, and we feel bad when they fail. Although these emotions can provide some learning benefits, in that they stimulate search processes, learning, and adaptation, they have been found to severely interfere with performance on tasks. In laboratory experiments, negative emotions have been found to interfere with an individual's allocation of attention in processing information. Such interference diminishes our ability to learn from the failure event.

For example, the negative emotional aspects of an event receive higher priority in processing information than positive or neutral emotional aspects. The emotional interference means that we prematurely terminate in working memory the facts that preceded the emotional event. But these facts are the basis for learning why the project failed. For example, in focusing on the emotional events leading up to the failure, our mind keeps shifting to the day the project was terminated. We dwell on the announcement to employees, buyers, suppliers, neighbors; how bad everyone felt; the moment of handing over the office keys to the liquidator and leaving the parking lot for the last time.

By focusing on these highly salient, emotional events, we do not allocate attention to information that would serve as important feedback for learning. Insufficient attention (and subsequently, diminished information processing capacity) is paid to the actions and inactions that caused the deterioration in performance and ultimately the project's failure. We all have limited attention and information processing capacity, and they are undercut by our emotional reactions. We enhance our learning when we manage our emotions and recover from our emotional pain more quickly. That is, we can manage our emotions to more quickly eliminate this source of interference in the learning process.

We enhance our learning when we manage our emotions and recover from our emotional pain more quickly.

We not only learn from failure the causes behind this specific event, but we learn and develop something special about ourselves. We also can personally grow from the experience.

"Success is a lousy teacher. It seduces smart people into thinking they can't lose."
—Bill Gates

"Mourning is not forgetting.... It is an undoing. Every minute tie has to be untied and something permanent and valuable recovered and assimilated from the dust. The end is gain, of course. Blessed are they that mourn, for they shall be made strong, in fact. But the process is like all other human births, painful and long and dangerous."
—Margery Allingham, The Tiger in the Smoke, 1956

CHAPTER 2

STRATEGIES TO LEARN MORE FROM YOUR FAILURES

The more someone is emotionally attached to a task, object, person, or activity, the more he or she experiences negative emotions when failure causes it to be lost. The process of mourning is painful and long and dangerous. In this chapter, you explore personal strategies for managing the emotions of failure so that the process of mourning is less painful and shorter and, in the end, a valuable learning experience. Mourning is not forgetting, but undoing. The personal strategies of this chapter help you "undo" the emotional ties to the project lost. At the same time, it empowers you to process information about the failure to learn

> *Mourning is not forgetting, but undoing.*

from the experience. The processing of mourning can even lead to a gain. It can make you stronger. It allows you to personally grow from the failure experience.

However, we don't always feel bad about a failure. Do we have such a negative emotional reaction to losing a small client—one who was costly to service with little upside potential? When it comes to feelings, not all failures are created equal. Before moving on to the strategies for managing emotions—so that mourning is less painful and shorter and leads to enhanced knowledge—you will explore why you feel worse over some failures than others. This discussion about why you feel emotional pain demonstrates that it is not the weak who feel this way—quite the contrary. Emotions arise in those who had the courage to emotionally commit to a project, to those who put it all on the line and gave it a go.

Project success depends on our commitment to it. The project begins with a creative idea, and we are more creative at projects to which we are passionately committed. But even highly creative ideas face obstacles to success that require high levels of commitment to working through these challenges. If you aren't committed to a project, it stands little chance of success.

❁

Why We Feel Bad over Project Failure

I use the label "project" to refer to tasks, relationships, activities, ventures, or businesses that form part of our work. These projects can fail. That is, they cease to exist. Project failure occurs when the project is terminated by key resource providers due to their assessment that the project's performance is unacceptably low. The "plug" can be "pulled" by others not directly involved in the project or by someone who is actively engaged. If the project was important, its loss due to failure generates a negative emotional reaction. The more important the project, the greater the reaction.[1] The greater the emotional reaction, the more important are the strategies and techniques offered in this chapter and the rest of the book for managing the process of bouncing back from failure, learning from the experience, and personally growing.

Why Some Projects Are More Important Than Others

As humans, we have a need to be satisfied.[2] We desire and seek out projects that make us feel good. Some projects satisfy these needs and make us feel good to a greater extent than others. The more a particular project satisfies a need, the better we feel—psychologically and physically. Therefore, the more a project satisfies our needs, the more important it is to us. This is not an objective measure of importance. Rather, it is highly subjective. What might be an important project to one person may be relatively unimportant to another. We feel bad when we lose something important to us.

The three primary needs are the need for competence, autonomy, and relatedness.

Figure 2.1 shows why we feel more or less bad after a project failure. We feel worse over a project's failure when that project satisfied our needs more than the project that took its place (the replacement project). The greater the loss of satisfaction arising from the failure, the worse we feel. Before moving on to strategies for managing emotions to make the mourning process less painful, shorter, and a positive learning experience, I'll delve deeper into how projects can satisfy our needs and, thus, how different projects generate emotional reactions that are more or less negative when they fail. The three primary needs are the need for competence, autonomy, and relatedness.[3]

How important is your current project to you? Or, how important to you was the project that just failed? Take the survey shown in Table 2.1. Then take your score for the competence subscale and put an X in the first column of Figure 2.2 in line with your score detailed on the y-axis. Do the same for the autonomy and relatedness subscales. If your X is in the white section of the column, you are high on this dimension. If it is in the light gray section, you are medium. If it is in the dark gray, you score low on this dimension. A high score on a subscale

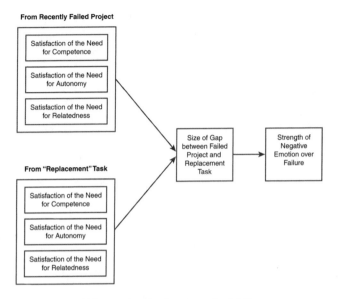

Figure 2.1   Why we feel bad over project failure

(in the white section) means that the project is (was) important to you. The more important a project is to you, the more you make the sorts of investments that increase its chances of success. But if it fails, you feel worse. *The more important the project, the greater the opportunity to learn, but also the greater the emotional obstacles to learning from the experience.* A medium score (light gray) means that the project is (was) of moderate importance to you. You feel somewhat bad if (when) the project fails (failed). A low score (dark gray) means that the project is (was) of low importance to you. You don't feel too bad when it fails. There are few obstacles to your learning from the failure so long as the learning task captures sufficient attention.

Table 2.1 How Important Is (Was) Your Project to You?[4]
To what extent do you agree that each statement reflects
your relationship with your current (or past) project?

Do Not Agree At All			Very Strongly Agree	
1	2	3	4	5

Competence Subscale

I feel that I make a substantial contribution toward progressing the project	1 2 3 4 5
I feel that I execute the project's tasks very effectively	1 2 3 4 5
I feel that this type of project and its tasks is one that I do very well	1 2 3 4 5
I feel that I can manage the requirements of my role in the project	1 2 3 4 5

Autonomy Subscale

This project is highly compatible with my choices and interests	1 2 3 4 5
I feel very strongly that the project tasks fit the way I prefer to work	1 2 3 4 5
I feel that how I work on the project is definitely an expression of myself	1 2 3 4 5
I feel very strongly that I have the opportunity to make choices with respect to how the project was undertaken	1 2 3 4 5

Relatedness Subscale

I feel extremely comfortable with the other members of the project team	1 2 3 4 5
I feel that I associate with the other team members in a very friendly way	1 2 3 4 5
I feel that there are open channels of communication with the other team members	1 2 3 4 5
I feel very much at ease with the other team members	1 2 3 4 5

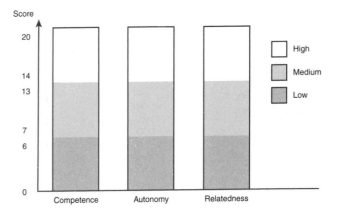

Figure 2.2 Chart your score for project importance

Some Projects Make Us Feel More Competent

If you scored high on the competence subscale of Table 2.1 (between 14 and 20, in the white section of column 1 in Figure 2.2), your project helps (helped) satisfy your psychological need for competence. If you had a medium score (7 to 13; light gray), the project somewhat satisfies your psychological need for competence. If you had a low score (0 to 6; dark gray), the project does little to satisfy your psychological need for competence.

A project satisfies your need for competence when by working on the project you receive feedback related to your skills, knowledge, and experience. The need for competence is satisfied if that feedback is positive. Positive feedback signals that your performance on project tasks is highly effective. This makes you feel satisfied. Alternatively, the

Positive feedback signals that your performance on project tasks is highly effective.

need for competence is satisfied if the feedback is developmental such that you feel you are building your skills, abilities, and/or knowledge by working on this project.

For example, Mike is a researcher who enjoys working with Chuck and Joy because they appreciate his attention to detail and the high-quality input into the research process. They provide him considerable positive feedback, which makes him feel good. On larger projects, Mike enjoys working with Denis and Larry, who are often critical of him for being slow and overly detailed on initial tests of an idea. This negative feedback highlights a weakness in Mike's research process that diminishes the quantity of his work. He feels good about this feedback because he can work on speeding up his process and thereby enhance his research abilities.

Projects that satisfy a need for competence can take many different forms. Some projects are structured in small "doable" steps so that as the steps are successfully completed, project team members receive positive performance feedback. In such instances, they build feelings of mastery of the task. They also develop a belief in their ability to successfully complete subsequent project tasks; that is, they build their self-belief related to the project. This self-belief is important because those who believe they will successfully complete a project are more likely to do so than those who have a less "firm" belief in themselves (even when they have the same knowledge, skills, experience, and abilities).

Most projects involve teams. A team can have a culture that helps satisfy your need for competence. For example, project teams that have a culture of constructive competition with others in the team or with other teams in the organization can promote feedback.[5] This feedback can be positive, satisfying the need for competence, and/or the feedback can be constructive, enabling the development of new knowledge, skills, and abilities, which also satisfies the need for competence. For example, two teams are developing a new video game in which the player feels as if he or she is riding a surfboard. In the case where a focus group indicates that team Alpha is superior to team Bravo in all dimensions, team Alpha receives positive feedback that satisfies its need for competence. But the feedback to team Bravo provides considerable information about how the team can improve the "reality" of their version of the surfing game and how to avoid the "artificiality" of the graphics in games they develop in the future. The team feels good about the competition and the feedback because it has improved its competence at game building. Furthermore, a team can develop a collective belief in its ability to successfully complete the project's tasks. The benefits of this collective belief are similar to those of self-belief. Collective belief is highly valued by its members because it helps satisfy their needs for competence.

However, when the project fails, this satisfaction is thwarted. Failure is often interpreted as negative feedback thwarting the need for competence. A failed project no longer provides the opportunity to develop your knowledge, skills, and abilities. When the project fails, the team usually is disbanded, and people are reassigned to different projects throughout the organization. The new project team may have a culture that does not promote constructive competition to the same extent and/or does not have the same high level of collective belief as the team of the failed project. In such a case, the project failure means that there are fewer opportunities to satisfy the need for competence. This diminished satisfaction triggers a negative emotional reaction. The greater the loss in satisfying the needs for competence brought about by the failure, the greater the emotional reaction.

Some Projects Makes Us Feel More in Control

If you got a high score on the autonomy subscale of Table 2.1 (between 14 and 20; in the white section of column 1 in Figure 2.2), your project helps (helped) satisfy your psychological need for autonomy/control. If you had a medium score (7 to 13; light gray), the project somewhat satisfies this psychological need. If you had a low score (0 to 6; dark gray), the project does little to satisfy your psychological need for autonomy/control.

A project satisfies our need for autonomy/control when it lets us decide when, where, and how to perform the project's tasks. We are less satisfied by projects when our activities, assignments, timing, access to resources, and so on are dictated by others or by the environmental conditions. We like to have personal control over our work-related activities.

Organizations that have more organic, informal structures allow those working closest to the "coal face" (where the action is) to exert personal control over how the project proceeds. When involved with projects that provide us more autonomy, we typically invest more in the project. For example, we use more of our knowledge and invest more of our time and energy in the project.[6] Autonomy provides us the freedom to think more about the project's tasks and the freedom to be more creative.[7] The additional commitment, other emotional investments, and creative thinking stimulated by a project's autonomy are often key to a project's success. Autonomy is also important for our well-being. We feel greater satisfaction and lower levels of stress when our project provides considerable autonomy.[8]

> *We feel greater satisfaction and lower levels of stress when our project provides considerable autonomy.*

However, when such a project fails and we are reassigned to a new project with less autonomy, our level of satisfaction is diminished. Failure has caused the loss of something important, and as a result, we feel bad. The greater the loss in autonomy caused by project failure, the greater the emotional reaction.

Some Projects Make Us Feel Like We Belong

If you got a high score on the relatedness subscale of Table 2.1 (between 14 and 20; in the white section of column 1 in Figure 2.2), your project helps (helped) satisfy your psychological need for relatedness and to belong. If you had a medium score (7 to 13; light gray), the project somewhat satisfies this psychological need. If you had a low score (0 to 6; dark gray), the project does little to satisfy your psychological need for relatedness and to belong.

We feel good when we are part of the team.

A project satisfies a need for relatedness by providing us a "link" to others. We feel good when we are part of the team. The members of the team are often linked by a common purpose. For the team to work well, its members must be "on the same track," have complementary skills, and continually communicate to maintain coordinated performance on project tasks. Working with others on a project can help build strong relational bonds among team members. These relationships make us feel like we belong and feel important. Indeed, a project may form part of our identity; those who work on the project are one of "us," and those who are not are one of "them."

We feel satisfied when we are related to others and when we feel like we belong. When a project that gives us these feelings of relatedness fails, we have lost something important, and we feel bad. We have negative feelings such as anxiety, loneliness, and diminished psychological and physical health.[9]

Strategize to Learn from Failure

Whether the project involves the development of new products, new processes, new ventures, or new businesses, these projects are often important to us, and we feel bad when they fail. As detailed in Chapter 1, "Managing Emotions to Learn from Failure," this period after failure can be emotionally painful, it can extend for a substantial period, and it represents a major obstacle to learning from the experience. Without learning, we do not have the opportunity to personally grow, and we are likely to make the same mistakes again.

Charlie Goetz represents a great example of learning from experiences. Charlie was a senior executive at Citicorp before pursuing a series of entrepreneurial ventures. He built nine businesses, three of which failed. When I spoke with Charlie, he recalled his first business:

> *"My first business failed. I was young. I was 26 years old. I basically had the idea that I was going to make millions. It was a restaurant in food courts in malls that sold French fries and sodas. So I opened three of them. I did this because all fast food restaurants basically make all their money from French fries and sodas. Therefore, why don't I just*

open up in a mall where they are selling everything else, and I'll provide the best French fries and I will also do sodas and I will give them a better price. I realized that the concept had a lot of validity, but there were little things that I never paid attention to. Everything seemed to be working well except for the concept of the people you could hire to manage it. Basically the people you are going to hire to work in the place are the people who are not going to show up. You assume they have the same business ethics that you do—but they don't. They need your constant attention. What should have been a very exciting and profitable concept did not work because of the people. The business was doing well, though. Revenues were beating projections; I just couldn't manage it. I ended up focusing on little things that I did not think were going to be important.

"I was very depressed. It was my first business. I had lost everything. I had only $200 to my name. I am one of these people who likes to be just left alone. One thing I am doing is thinking. For the first two weeks I am thinking about why it happened. What I could have done differently. In the next two weeks I start to think about what do I do now. What is my next logical step in this situation? You learn from your failures when you can really step back and analyze them. Hopefully you analyze why they failed."

Charlie began by trying to make sense of why the business had failed. But then he took the necessary steps to address secondary causes of stress— loss of income—and rebuild his life. Once his life was back on track, he was able to turn his thoughts back to the business failure and more objectively analyze why it had failed. Charlie believes that learning from your experiences is vitally important: "No doubt you learn much more from your failures than your successes. I have built nine businesses, and three have failed. The batting average is not bad. But those failures—I learned more from them than all the successes. I enjoy the successes more; don't kid yourself. But you can learn a lot of lessons from those failures."

For Charlie Goetz, learning from failure is not automatic or instantaneous; rather, it involves a process of managing the emotions generated from the failure event. There are three strategies for managing these emotions. The first strategy is to focus attention on the failure and "work through the loss" to create a plausible account for the failure and thereby reduce negative emotions. The second strategy is focused on restoration. It shifts attention away from the loss to address secondary causes of stress to reduce the generation of negative emotions. Both these strategies have pros and cons in helping us manage our emotions to learn from failure and grow from the experience. The third strategy involves oscillating between the other two strategies. For example, you could use the first strategy and then the second and then back to the first and keep alternating until you have learned from the experience. This oscillation (alternating) strategy allows us to benefit from the pros of the other two strategies while minimizing the cons. I will now detail each strategy.

An Emotion-Management Strategy of "Working Through the Loss"

This learning strategy is to orient yourself on the failure and work through the experience to try and make sense of what happened. By focusing on the events surrounding the failure, we can find new information about what caused it. By processing this information, we can learn new knowledge. We can adjust how we think about projects and how we act when working on new projects. To the extent we have learned from the failure experience, we can avoid making the same mistakes again. This strategy is referred to as "working through the loss" because it is not an easy process; it requires mental and emotional work.

It helps to talk with family, friends, and colleagues.

In using this strategy, we focus on the events surrounding the project's failure. We think about the different courses of action we could have taken and how these different paths would have led to different outcomes. We think about the factors that were critical to the project's demise. These can include actions we took, actions we failed to take, changes in the external environment that were ignored, and anticipated changes in the environment that did not materialize.

For example, in working through the losses of project failure, it helps to talk with family, friends, and colleagues. By talking about the events surrounding the failure, we bring out in the open our underlying assumptions about the failure and its causes. By bringing them into the open and "putting them on the table," we can better assess their plausibility. Our confidants can help us make sense of the failure by highlighting useful information, implausible assumptions, and what pieces of the puzzle are missing. By working through the loss, we search for more information and process it to construct a plausible explanation for the failure. As we go through this process of creating a series of accounts for the project's failure that become more and more plausible, we gain a deeper understanding of why the loss occurred. This understanding makes us think differently about ourselves, our projects, and even the world around us. As we gain a deeper understanding of why our project failed, we can break our emotional bonds to it. The failure is no longer seen as a totally unexplained event.

❁

For example, Don Jackson undertook the project of gaining a major donation to keep the Stamp Out Hunger outreach program for the poor in operation. This program provided nutritious food to a local shelter. The project failed. Not only did Don fail to add a new donor, but he also lost a smaller donor in the process, and the outreach program had to be ended. As a result, fewer poor people received the help they needed. Don felt awful. He constructed an account of what went wrong. His approach was too confrontational, he waited too long to try to raise money, and the drop in the stock market meant that wealthy individuals were not as forth-coming with donations. Knowing why he failed to raise money for the charity made him feel a little better. At least he realized he could do some things differently next time—use a more collaborative approach, start the process earlier, and gain com-mitments when the economic cycle is good. But he also took some comfort in the fact that there was little he could do about the larger economic condi-tions. With the anxiety of not knowing what caused the failure gone, Don could begin emotionally with-drawing from the failed outreach program and com-mit to the next project.

However, there are some costs to using this strategy to manage emotions to learn from the fail-ure experience. Working through the loss requires us to confront the failure head on. Focusing our attention on the events surrounding the failure and thinking about the loss can make negative thoughts and memories more salient. For example, Don began to focus on the poor children who would not receive a nutritious meal that day, their increased susceptibility to illness, and the anxiety their parents must feel about not being able to provide for them. In other words, when we think about the causes of failure, our thoughts can easily move to the conse-quences of failure. For example, thinking about the team's actions may trigger memories of the special bond that existed between team members and how bad everyone felt when the project failed and the team was disbanded. Such memories exacerbate our negative emotions.[10] They can even lead to ruminations—thoughts and emotions that build off each other to escalate the emotional obstacles to learning from failure. For example, we start thinking about how bad we felt when the project failed, which makes us feel bad now, which makes us think about how bad the other team members must feel now, which makes us feel worse. These emotions interfere with our ability to search for, and process, information about the project failure, which decreases our ability to learn from the experience.

❁

The strategy of working through the loss has a number of pros and cons. The pros of the "working through the loss" strategy include the following:

- It helps focus attention on collecting information about why the project failed.
- It encourages us to talk through the loss with others, which helps us construct a series of more plausible accounts of the project failure.
- As we develop more meaning behind the project failure, we can break the emotional bonds to the project that was lost.
- As we break emotional bonds to the project that was lost, we minimize negative emotions and eventually eliminate them.

The cons of "working through the loss" are as follows:

- When we focus on the events surrounding the project's failure, our thoughts can turn to its consequences and the emotions surrounding the failure.
- Confronting the loss can be emotionally exhausting.
- Working through the loss can lead to ruminations that escalate negative emotions (rather than reduce them) and interfere with our ability to collect and process the new information necessary to learn from the experience.

An Emotion-Management Strategy of Restoration

Another strategy for managing the emotions involved with project failure is to "restore" ourselves. This strategy has two prongs: avoidance and being proactive toward secondary causes of stress.

This strategy has two prongs: avoidance and being proactive toward secondary causes of stress.

The first prong, avoidance, allows us to stop thinking about the project and its failure. By not thinking about the project failure, we can minimize our negative feelings. We can use distractions to achieve this avoidance. That is, when we throw ourselves into other tasks, our attention is occupied, and our mind is unavailable to think about the failure and therefore unavailable to generate emotions. For example, by fully focusing on a new project at work, the garden, or a football game, the mind does not have the chance to generate these emotions.

The second prong of the restoration strategy is being proactive toward secondary causes of stress triggered by the project failure. Bill Lewis, who founded eight businesses and went through two bankruptcies, said that the loss of his business was devastating. He lost not only his company, but also his home. He believed he had lost everything, including his income, his social status, and his belief in his ability to be successful at work. These consequences of failure caused him stress (over and above the loss of satisfaction of his needs for competence, autonomy, and relatedness). Indeed, it was so overwhelming that he felt he could not handle it. At this moment in time Bill did not need to focus on the events surrounding the losses. Instead, he needed to distract himself from such thoughts and take action to start rebuilding his life.

By taking action to resolve the problems caused by the failure of his business, Bill can eliminate the secondary stressors. For example, he might apply for a new job, socially network, and take smaller steps on a new assignment to ensure positive performance feedback. That is, we focus on addressing the problems that were caused by the failure rather than focusing on the failure itself. In a way this is a distraction task, but it can also reduce the negative impact of the project failure. This being proactive involves putting other aspects of your life back on track and maintaining essential activities. As secondary causes of stress are eliminated, the primary cause of stress—the project failure—will not loom as large. Thoughts of the project failure will generate a weaker emotional reaction, and thus there will be fewer obstacles to learning from the experience.

However, this strategy also has some limitations. When you distract yourself from the project failure, no attention is focused on collecting new information about why the project failed, no processing of the information about the project failure occurs, and thus no learning takes place. This means that the mistakes that caused the project failure might happen again. It is also important to note that it is difficult to use this strategy for an extended period. It is difficult to *not* think about an important event for a long time, and this also has its costs. Suppressing emotion can be exhausting and can have negative physical consequences, such as headaches and ulcers. Indeed, eventually these emotions resurface. When they do, the grieving process is more painful, takes longer, and presents more obstacles to learning.

❁

The strategy of restoration has a number of pros and cons. Here are the pros:

- By avoiding thinking about the project failure, fewer negative emotions are generated.
- Avoidance gives us time to subconsciously deal with the loss.

- Addressing secondary causes of stress enables us to begin to restructure our work and our lives to prepare for the next, new phase at work.

- As we reduce secondary causes of stress, the primary cause of stress—the business failure—does not loom as large and generates a weaker emotional reaction.

The cons of the restoration strategy are as follows:

- With attention focused on distracter tasks, little scanning and interpretation of information surrounds the project failure, so no learning occurs.

- If the distracter task is another project, we may be doomed to make the same mistake again, causing this project to fail also.

- It is difficult to suppress negative emotions for an extended period, and there is often a psychological and physical cost in doing so.

- When suppressed emotions resurface, the impact can be more negative.

So far I have described two strategies for managing the emotions generated by project failure. Both offer a number of benefits, but each also has a number of costs. These costs arise from using either of the strategies for an extended period of time. The next strategy is a combination of the two strategies such that neither is used for an extended period.

Joe Bambridge is an example of someone who used both strategies at different times to manage his emotions to learn from failure. Joe left his job with a consulting firm to start his own business. Central to the success of this business was an alliance relationship with another firm. He describes how he felt when the relationship failed and how he tried to manage those emotions:

> "We made a start. But after a couple years it became clear to me that the relationship would fall apart. It hit me hard. I had to basically go reinvent myself on-the-fly very quickly in order to keep generating income. [During the breakup of the alliance relationship] I was surprised to find that I felt a lot of anxiety. This was a new thing for me. I would receive some email about the failing relationship, and there was definitely an emotional outcome. This was a distraction. One time I had just gotten an email about the relationship termination, and the phone rang, and it was someone completely unrelated to this aspect of the business, and I picked up the phone and answered it like I used to do in my corporate career two or three years ago. I had never done that. It was like I was so flustered that my brain just went to the wrong place. It was distracting my focus. I was trying to focus on project A, but I felt this was distracting me off it in a direction that was not productive.

"At times like this I would go outside to get away from work. Part of it was to disconnect. I did not know what to do. But I found it was helpful to go and detach from everything for five or ten minutes. I then tried to push forward on other things that I could control.

"Taking a break would help. Sometimes talking helped. I had a significant other at the time, and I benefited greatly talking with her about it and what had happened and what I was doing now so that it would not happen again. It helped me focus on how to set up the next thing and how to protect myself from this happening again. So at least I would learn something. I also talked to my dad, who pointed out the emotional costs of alternate termination strategies. This helped a great deal."

It appears that Joe realized the benefits of a restoration orientation (taking a break and also moving on to other tasks that were under his control). But he also realized the benefits of talking through the failure and his emotions with others to ensure that he learned from his failure experience. In the next section, I discuss how we can use both a restoration and a "working through the loss" strategy to more effectively learn from failure and personally grow from the experience.

The Optimal Strategy: Oscillation

A strategy of oscillation for managing emotions surrounding project failure involves moving between using the "working through the loss" and "restoration" strategies.[11] By moving from one strategy to the other and back again as part of a continuous process, we can gain the benefits of each strategy while minimizing the costs of each. This allows us to more effectively manage our emotions such that the process is less painful, takes less time, and results in learning new knowledge.

To illustrate this strategy, consider the example of Joe, who had a negative emotional reaction to the failure of a relationship that was key to his business. I propose that Joe can start by working through the loss. He focuses on the events surrounding the failure. He focuses on the criteria used to select the partner in the first place, how the relationship formed, how it was contractually documented, the discussions about each person's expectations, the time spent getting to know each other, and so on. That is, during this period of working through the loss, we scan for potentially useful information and process available information to begin putting together pieces of the puzzle. The more pieces of the puzzle we have, and the more they are pieced together, the clearer the picture we have of how and why the project failed. As we develop a deeper understanding of the causes of the failure, we can break some of our emotional ties to the project. In Joe's case, he started to understand why the relationship failed and how his actions and inactions contributed to the failure. When you gain such an understanding, the emotional ties to the alliance (and the form of the business that was dependent on it) start to break.

Eventually, as we work through the loss, our attention begins to shift to the consequences of the failure and to how bad we felt. For example, Joe started to remember how bad he felt when he heard from the alliance partner that they were dissatisfied with the relationship. He thought about how the rejection of him as a partner made him feel like a failure, how tough it would be to secure the clients necessary to be successful at this career, and the embarrassment of having to tell people in the office (and at his previous job) that his strategic alliance had fallen apart. These negative memories and emotions start to consume our mental capacity, diminishing our ability to process information about the project failure. That is, memories and emotions take up some of the mental capacity we need to find pieces of the puzzle and put them together. As a result, we make little progress in understanding the causes of the project's failure, and we begin to feel worse and worse. Joe begins to feel depressed and sad. Even though he continues to work through the details of how best to sever the relationship, these activities only make him feel worse, because he is not in a state that allows him to learn. His mental gas tank is running on empty.

It is now that we shift to a "restoration" strategy. We turn our attention away from the project failure and focus it on other aspects of our lives. We throw ourselves into other activities to occupy our minds. For example, Joe puts aside emails related to the alliance and goes to a football game with friends. He cheers for his team and shouts advice to the coaches, players, and referees. This helps break the cycle of continuously thinking about the negative aspects of the failed alliance (project failure). This sort of distraction gives us a chance to recharge our cognitive batteries. By focusing our attention elsewhere, we take a break from working through the loss and reduce our negative feelings. We also begin taking steps toward restructuring our work and our lives by addressing the problems generated by the project failure. For example, Joe goes back to the office but works on other aspects of his job. These actions will reduce secondary causes of stress, because there are now fewer things on his to-do list. In doing so, dealing with the repercussions of an alliance gone bad is no longer as daunting.

As soon as our mental batteries have been recharged, we can switch back to working through the loss. Given that we have eliminated some of the secondary stressors, as our attention returns to the project failure, its negative impact does not seem nearly so large. We gather and process more information and construct a clearer picture of the project failure. This allows us to further break the emotional bonds to the project. For example, Joe can once again turn his attention to understanding the partner's reaction and making necessary changes to his planned approach to another alliance partner. As this understanding increases, Joe further breaks the emotional bonds to the original project.

As thoughts eventually move to the consequences of failure and generate emotions, this strategy becomes less effective, and we feel emotionally exhausted. At this point in time, we switch back to a "restoration" strategy. Joe might turn to his other duties or go to lunch with friends. We continue with this process of oscillation until thoughts of the project failure no longer generate a negative emotional reaction that interferes with our normal functioning. This oscillation strategy manages failure in a way that minimizes the emotional pain, maximizes learning, and more quickly eliminates the emotional pain.

Figure 2.3 illustrates the oscillation strategy. The failure of an important project generates an emotional reaction, which is painful, takes time to recover from, and obstructs learning. A process of oscillating between the two strategies can enhance our ability to learn from failure and personally grow from the experience.

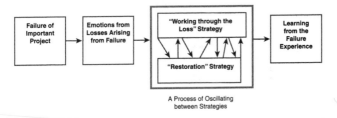

A Process of Oscillating
between Strategies

Figure 2.3 The strategy of oscillation to manage emotions and learn from failure

❁

The benefits of the oscillation strategy are the benefits of the other two strategies:

■ It helps focus attention on collecting information about why the project failed.

- It encourages us to talk through the loss with others, which helps us construct a series of more plausible accounts of the project failure.

- As we develop more meaning behind the project failure, we can break the emotional bonds to the project lost.

- As we bring emotional bonds to the project lost, we minimize the emotional reaction and eventually eliminate it.

- By avoiding thinking about the project failure, we generate fewer negative emotions.

- Avoidance gives us time to subconsciously deal with the loss.

- Addressing secondary causes of stress enables us to begin restructuring our work and our lives to prepare for the next, new phase of work.

- As we reduce secondary causes of stress, the primary cause of stress—the business failure—does not loom as large and generates a weaker emotional response.

Conclusion

Projects differ in how important they are to us. Projects that better satisfy our needs for competence, autonomy, and relatedness are more important. The more important the project, the greater the emotional reaction when it fails. This emotional reaction is painful, it takes time to recover, and the reaction obstructs learning. We can act in ways to lessen the pain, shorten the recovery period, and learn more from the failure to personally grow from the experience.

One strategy focuses on working through the loss to construct meaning behind a failure. In doing so, the emotional bonds are broken such that further thoughts of the failure no longer raise a negative emotional reaction. However, continuously focusing on the events surrounding the failure can be emotionally exhausting. Thoughts eventually turn to the consequences of the failure, thereby increasing our emotional reaction.

An alternative strategy is restoration, which involves distracting your thoughts from the project failure to avoid generating emotions. It also involves actively solving other problems generated by the project failure. If you address the secondary causes of stress, the project failure itself will seem less daunting. But the restoration strategy involves suppressing emotion, which is difficult to do over an extended period. Avoidance does little to promote learning from the experience.

> *Avoidance does little to promote learning from the experience.*

The optimal strategy is oscillation, which involves continuously switching between the other two strategies. It provides the same benefits as the other two strategies while minimizing their costs. The oscillation strategy can help us reduce the emotional pain of project failure and shorten the amount of time we feel this pain. It also enhances our ability to learn and grow from the failure experience.

❄

Endnotes

1 Shepherd, D.A. and Cardon, M. "Negative emotional reactions to project failure and the self-compassion to learn from the experience." *Journal of Management Studies* (forthcoming).

2 Ryan, R.M. and Deci, E.L. (2000). "Self-determination theory and the facilitation of intrinsic motivation, social development, and well-being." *American Psychologist*, 55: 68–78.

3 Ibid.

4 Adapted from Vlachopoulos, S.P. and Michailidou, S. (2006). "Development and initial validation of a measure of autonomy, competence, and relatedness in exercise: The basic needs in exercise scale." *Measurement in Physical Education and Exercise Science*, 10(3): 179–201.

5 Tjosvold, D., Johnson, D.W., Johnson, R.T., and Sun, H. (2003). "Can interpersonal competition be constructive within organizations?" *Journal of Psychology*, 11137(1): 63–84.

6 O'Driscoll, M.P., Pierce, J.L., and Coghlan, A.M. (2006). "The psychology of ownership." *Group and Organization Management*, 31(3): 388–416.

7 Amabile, T.M. (1982). "Social psychology of creativity: A consensual assessment technique." *Journal of Personality and*

Social Psychology, 43: 997–1013; Grolnick, W.S. and Ryan, R.M. (1987). "Autonomy in children's learning: An experimental and individual difference investigation." *Journal of Personality and Social Psychology*, 52: 890–898.

8 Deci, E.L., Schwartz, A.J., Sheinman, L., and Ryan, R.M. (1981). "An instrument to assess adults' orientations toward control versus autonomy with children: Reflections on intrinsic motivation and perceived competence." *Journal of Educational Psychology*, 73: 642–650; Hackman, J.R. and Oldham, G.R. (1980). *Work Redesign*. Reading, MA: Addison-Wesley; Purasuraman, S. and Alutto, J.A. (1984). "Sources and outcomes of stress in organizational settings: Toward the development of a structural model." *Academy of Management Journal*, 27(2): 330–350.

9 Baumeister, R.F. and Tice, D.M. (1990). "Anxiety and social exclusion." *Journal of Social and Clinical Psychology*, 9: 165–195; DeLongis, A., Folkman, S., and Lazarus, R.S. (1988). "The impact of daily stress on health and mood: Psychological and social resources as mediators." *Journal of Personality and Social Psychology*, 54(3): 486–495.

10 Wortman, C.B. and Silver, R.C. (1987). "Coping with irrevocable loss." In G.R. Van de Bos and B.K. Bryant (eds.), *Cataclysms, Crises and Catastrophes: Psychology in Action* 189–235. Washington D.C.: American Psychological Association.

11 Shepherd, D.A. (2003). "Learning from business failure: Propositions about the grief recovery process for the self-employed." *Academy of Management Review*, 28: 318–329; Stroebe, M.S. and Schut, H. (1999). "The oscillation of coping with bereavement: Rationale and description." *Death Studies*, 23: 197–224.

"THERE IS NO TERROR IN THE BANG,
ONLY IN THE ANTICIPATION OF IT."
—*ALFRED HITCHCOCK*

"SUCCESS IS NOT FINAL, FAILURE IS
NOT FATAL: IT IS THE COURAGE TO
CONTINUE THAT COUNTS."
—*SIR WINSTON CHURCHILL*

Chapter 3

The emotional reaction to a failure does not occur only at the time of the failure event. As you explored in the previous chapter, the emotions triggered by project failure can linger long after the event to obstruct learning. You can use the oscillation approach (going back and forth from "working through" to "restoration") to manage these "post-failure" emotions so that they are less painful and shorter and provide the basis of a valuable learning experience. However, emotions can be triggered even in anticipation of an event.

In this chapter, I discuss the emotions triggered by the anticipation of failure and how these emotions should be considered when you're thinking about finally "pulling the plug" on a failing project. This decision to "pull the plug" is a difficult but important one because it affects your ability to emotionally and financially grow from the failure experience. We often know when a project is performing poorly. The question is not whether it will fail, but when. Despite knowing that a project is failing and won't recover, it is very difficult to "kill" it, to put the final "nail in the coffin," to "pull the plug" on its life support system. Because of this reluctance to pull the plug and trigger the failure event, we often persist with this losing course of action. We are not alone in doing so. Many people, across a range of projects, "throw good money after bad" even in the face of mounting evidence that the project is performing poorly, will not recover, and will eventually fail. The consequences can be dire. Take the example of Jeff Schwartz:[1]

> Jeff Schwartz is proudly demonstrating his company's most popular product: a framed photograph of the U.S. hockey team defeating the Soviets in the 1980 Olympics. Push the button at the bottom of the frame and Al Michaels' memorable words come crackling out of a tiny speaker. For a few fleeting seconds, the Miracle on Ice comes to life.
>
> It's not quite enough to give you the chills, but almost. The company's modest offices, near the breakers in the leafy beach town of San Clemente, Calif., are festooned with these talking frames—tributes, mostly, to sportsmen persevering and triumphing in the face of impossible odds. There's an echoing

Lou Gehrig ("I consider myself the luckiest man...man...man...on the face of the earth...earth...earth."), Bobby Thomson, and Jackie Robinson. Schwartz circles around his desk to demonstrate another of his favorites. But this time, when he presses the button, no sound comes out. "The batteries must have died on these things," he says brusquely, "they've been sitting here so long."

It's a jarring reminder of why we're here— not to play with the merchandise (which is undeniably appealing), but because Jeff Schwartz's business, Remarkable Moments, has failed. Schwartz, 43, is standing amidst the accumulated detritus of five years of unsuccessful endeavor: empty frames, piles of inventory, and snarls of partially disassembled sound-editing equipment. Out back, his wife, Sandy, is about to start loading things into a Ryder truck to be hauled off. It is, in a macabre kind of way, a remarkable moment.

But what's really bugging Schwartz isn't that he's pulling the plug on his dream. It's that he didn't pull the plug long ago—before he had gone almost three years without a salary. Before he had burned through another $100,000 of his own money (the dividend of a previous successful company he had sold). Before Sandy quit the PTA and other

*community activities because of the busi-
ness's demands. Before he had run out of
money even to pay his two children for their
efforts. Before he had raided their college
funds. "And the biggest thing I've lost isn't
the money. It's five years or so," broods
Schwartz, his eyes downcast. "I could have
played golf and watched TV for the last five
years, and I'd have more money than I do
now."*

He means that literally. He's done the math.

We often think of persistence and determination as personal qualities. With great determination, we persist in the face of obstacles and often can work our way through the tough times and ultimately achieve success. But for terminal projects—those that are destined to fail—this attribute of determination and persistence can become a financial liability. By persistence we delay the inevitable, and this delay is costly. Delaying project failure is costly because we still invest time, money, and energy into a project that will not create a sufficient financial return on that investment. It is also costly because while we are investing our resources, including attention, into this project, we are investing less in other existing projects and perhaps not seeing opportunities for new projects. To continue with the example of Jeff Schwartz, this perplexing reality that persistence and determination can increase the likelihood that you are successful also increases the costs of failure by encouraging you to delay pulling the plug:

Like everyone else, he'd [Jeff Schwartz] been schooled in the Vince Lombardi-style slogans that cloak entrepreneurial lore. That winners never quit. That quitters never win. That, in the oft-quoted line from the movie Apollo 13, "Failure is not an option." Yet now experience seems to have taught him a different lesson. "The blinders-on, full-speed-ahead mentality sounds great, and it really does motivate people," says Schwartz. "But the sad truth is that 'never give up' isn't always the right thing. For people like me, it means we burn through our savings.... My failure wasn't in taking the risk to start the company; it was when I let it bleed my family dry." Pausing, he asks: "When does your ally—tenacity—become your worst enemy?" ... But do not be deluded: failure is an option, and in some instances it's the wisest option there is.

So delaying "pulling the plug" of a failing project can be costly. Jeff Schwartz lost five years of his life and an additional $100,000, and his family had also made major sacrifices. So why did Jeff do it? Why do we delay failure when doing so makes failure more financially costly when it

Why do we delay failure when doing so makes failure more financially costly when it eventually occurs?

eventually occurs? And, consequently, when the failure makes our paths to personal growth longer and more difficult? In other words, why do we go down the same path of delaying failure as Jeff Schwartz did even though it is financially costly to do so?

❄

Charlie Goetz, who has experienced three business failures, provides some insight into the thinking and emotions behind terminating a failing project:

> "I have never had a business that had failed out of left field. I knew it was coming. Things weren't working right. In the beginning I'd work out the problem and I'd solve it and then I'd come across another problem. But eventually I'd get to the point where the problems were coming faster than I could solve them and it was only a matter of time until I came to the resolution that this was not going to work. I know I kept the business going longer than I economically should have.

> "That is the problem. As you start to see things going down, you know it. You really know it. But you say, 'Let's try it. Let's give it a shot. Let's do this and let's do that.' Normally, when you are doing good business, you try and hit singles and doubles, but now that things aren't working, you are trying to hit triples and home runs. And then

you are really in bad trouble. Maybe you will get very lucky. But the odds aren't good. And most of the time the failure is inevitable. But unfortunately a lot of the people in the firm don't believe it.

"I delayed [pulling the plug on the business] because there is an emotional attachment.

"While it is an entity, it is a living entity, and there is a relationship not only with the people there but the business itself. It is part of who you are. You put all your passion into it. This is what makes us entrepreneurs successful—the passion. You believe in it so much that it is hard to say, 'You know, I was wrong.'"

❄

There are three possible explanations for why we deviate from the economic rule of thumb and delay failure:[2]

- We do so because our decisions are biased and are made in error.
- We procrastinate because of the short-term costs of negative emotions.
- The delay provides a period of anticipatory processing that enhances our emotional recovery.

It is important to recognize those situations when our approach is biased or involves decision errors, because this provides us the opportunity to improve our decision making—not to get "sucked in" by the situation and make bad decisions. It is also important to acknowledge that we feel emotions from failure. They should be acknowledged in our approach to pulling the plug to enhance our learning from failure and the motivation to move on to the next project.

Are We Biased When We Delay Failure?

A common explanation for why decision makers stick with a course of action despite its poor performance is the notion of *escalation of commitment*. This refers to an increasing commitment to the same course of action in a sequence of decisions resulting in negative outcomes.[3] We escalate commitment for a number of reasons. It is like losing at gambling in Las Vegas and playing on in an effort to win back what was lost. First, we may persist with a losing course of action to justify previous decisions. Deciding to terminate the failing project would be a decision that undermines previous decisions to start the project in the first place and subsequent decisions to persist with it. It

> *It is difficult to decide to terminate a project when doing so invalidates previous decisions.*

is difficult to decide to terminate a project when doing so invalidates previous decisions. Of course, the decision to terminate now based on new information does not necessarily invalidate previous decisions to persist based on the information at the time, but people often perceive it this way.

We may also persist with a failing endeavor to justify our previous decisions to others. Business people typically are overconfident about their chances of success. In a survey of 2,994 business founders, one study found that 81% of these entrepreneurs believed that their venture's chance of success was over 70%, and one third believed that the likelihood of success was 100%. (Realistic expectations are in the range of 30 to 70%.)[4] This overconfidence influences the representations entrepreneurs make to others, such as equity investors as well as family and friends. Failure repudiates the representations we have made to others about the project's prospects. By delaying failure, the individual does not repudiate previous representations (to himself or herself or to others)—at least for the time being. Therefore, the decision to delay failure can be biased based on a need to justify previous decisions to self and/or others.

❁

Perhaps Jeff Schwartz delayed pulling the plug on the business because coming to that determination would invalidate the other business decisions he had made up to that point. It would invalidate his business plan—that the marketing research showing the "overwhelming latent demand" for sports memorabilia was flawed. It would invalidate his earlier decision to source the memorabilia in the United States rather than China. It would invalidate his decision to use debt funding rather than forming a strategic alliance with a sporting goods retailer. By delaying the decision to pull the plug, he was able to avoid invalidating his previous decisions (at least for the time being). Indeed, the decision to persist was consistent with his past decisions that reflected a belief in the viability of the business.

It is also likely that Jeff was initially confident in the success of Remarkable Memories, especially given the success of his previous business. Given this confidence, he made representations to others, including his wife and family, but also probably to bankers and employees. Delaying the decision to pull the plug on the business is consistent with, and does not invalidate, these previous representations to others.

Second, we may delay failure and persist with a poorly performing project because we over-generalize the "don't waste" decision rule.[5] Because we have invested considerable time, energy, and money into the project, the decision to terminate it would mean that the previous investments of valuable resources were wasted. This is commonly referred to as the "sunk cost" effect. *Sunk costs* are investments made in a project that are unrecoverable.

Take the case of two managers responsible for the development and launch of a new product. The first manager, Rachael, led the project from the beginning. The second manager, Elaina, was also responsible for the launch of her company's new product, but she had only recently taken over leadership of the project from its founder, Jim. Research has shown that managers, such as Rachael, who have been with the project from the beginning have a stronger relationship with their projects than managers like Elaina, who take over a project later. Relative to Elaina, Rachael was more committed to her project, was more active in accelerating the development of her project, and continued to fund the project despite poor performance. Rachael lost more of the firm's resources on her project failure than did Elaina.[6]

When making a decision about future investments, sunk costs should not be considered in the decision. The decision should be based solely on the return of resources currently being considered for investing. For Jeff Schwartz, regardless of how much money and time he had already invested in this business, the investment of more resources needed to be based on what future returns could be gained from this investment. Prior investments of time and money are sunk—they are not coming back and therefore should not enter into his decision of whether to invest the additional $100,000. Although sunk costs should not be considered, they often are, and across a whole range of decision contexts.

Third, the termination or persistence decision represents accepting a certain loss in place of an uncertain loss. By terminating the project, we accept the loss now and know what its cost is. When we delay failure, we are uncertain how much

When we delay failure, we are uncertain how much the cost of failure will be.

the cost of failure will be. Despite the financial cost of failure from immediate termination being known and lower than the expected cost of delaying failure, people often take this risk. When we are in a loss situation, we can seek risk—and we choose the riskier alternative despite the expected cost being higher.[7] You might see this phenomenon in a casino where the woman next to you is up (she has more chips than she started with), and she begins to put chips in her pocket and bet more conservatively. The man on the other side of you is in a loss situation (he has only half the chips he started with), and he begins to take greater risks to win back his money by, for example, doubling down. It could be that realizing that his business was failing, Jeff Schwartz doubled down by investing additional money in a highly risky strategy—for example, moving manufacturing offshore—as one last shot (a "hail Mary") to recoup his losses. Of course, if it does not work, the failure is now more costly than it needed to be.

It could be that it is not so much that we seek risk, but that we hold out hope that the project will turn around and become successful (despite the odds). However, in laboratory experiments where there is no uncertainty that the activity is a losing course of action—they know they will be economically worse off by persisting—some people continue to do so. Therefore, despite knowing that their project will fail and that additional investments will increase the financial cost of failure, some individuals still delay failure. The economic basis for explaining the decision to delay failure does not provide adequate insight into why people's decision processes lead them to such a negative financial outcome. We need to complement the economic rule of thumb with an understanding of emotions in the process. Procrastination offers a dominant emotion-based explanation for delaying failure.

Are We Procrastinators?

Procrastination refers to postponing an action that is emotionally unattractive even though this action will lead to positive outcomes in the future.[8] You know that failure generates a negative emotional reaction. In anticipation of these

> *Procrastination is a self-defense mechanism we often use when we face a threat.*

emotions, you may delay failure to postpone this emotionally unattractive outcome. You also know that terminating a failing project reduces the financial cost of failure and provides the positive outcome in the future of a speedier financial recovery—you can more quickly engage in a subsequent project. Why, then, would you forgo a short-term emotional "hit" when the future financial costs of doing so are so great?

Procrastination is a self-defense mechanism we often use when we face a threat. You deal with the emotional threat of a failure by avoiding the situation and thereby avoiding the "appropriate" response to the threat of a failing project. Just thinking about the emotions that will be generated by failure creates anxiety and stress. By avoiding thinking about the decision to terminate the project, you can diminish your anxiety and distress. This reduction of anxiety and distress feels good and reinforces the avoidance strategy. You establish a pattern of avoidance behavior—one that is tough to break.

Procrastination is more likely and more deeply entrenched for events in which the anticipated negative emotions to be generated are the greatest. Although there are differences across individuals and across projects, failure often generates a considerably negative emotional reaction.

Procrastination is also more likely when the decision is irreversible. The anxiety and distress over the anticipation of a negative emotional reaction to "pulling the plug" are also high because when an entrepreneur closes a specific business or a manager terminates a specific project, the decision is irreversible. Procrastination is more likely and more entrenched for such irreversible decisions.

We often believe that success is within our control. Even though there are attempts to attribute blame for failure to others to maintain high self-esteem, we often still feel personally responsible for the outcome. Procrastination is more likely and more embedded when we feel more personally responsible for the outcome.

Perhaps Jeff Schwartz delayed pulling the plug on his business because he procrastinated over the decision. He anticipated that pulling the plug would be emotionally painful. Thinking about the business failing made him feel sick. Once the plug was pulled, that was it. It was all over. The business could not be resurrected. By putting off thinking about the decision, he was able to avoid that "sick to the stomach" feeling. It felt good to avoid thinking about the end. This encouraged him so that every time his thoughts turned to the possibility of pulling the plug, he could make himself feel better immediately by distracting himself from these thoughts. As this occurs repeatedly, the decision to pull the plug is delayed repeatedly.

Anticipatory Processing to Personally Grow from the Failure Experience

Most people engaged in projects are forewarned of failure (by others or by the accumulating evidence of poor performance) before the event actually takes place. "Anticipatory processing" is not only stimulated by being forewarned of the loss of the project. It also is stimulated by awareness of losses that have already occurred or are occurring now as a result of the project's failing state. For example, perhaps Jeff Schwartz pined over the loss of a vibrant business as it started slipping into decline. He grieved over the loss of his dreams for the project's future that would never be realized. Although anticipatory processing cannot completely emotionally prepare us for the failure event, it does provide a small taste of what it will be like when failure occurs.

Some management and accounting tools provide information about performance and even thresholds that, once breached, indicate a very high likelihood of project failure. (These include financial distress and bankruptcy models for businesses and stage gate objectives for projects.) Considerable information about a project's poor performance forewarns us of the upcoming failure event.

> *Awareness that the business or project will fail involves realizing that no "white knight" will ride in at the last minute and save the day.*

Forewarning of failure is a necessary but insufficient condition for anticipatory processing. Anticipatory processing requires us to accept that the project will fail and requires us to engage in some "working through the loss." Awareness that the business or project will fail involves realizing that no "white knight" will ride in at the last minute and save the day. We also realize that a different strategy or different level of effort can't turn this around and steer it away from failure. These possibilities have already been exhausted.

Anticipatory processing does not require that we continuously engage in "working through the loss." Indeed, as discussed in Chapter 2, "Strategies to Learn More from Your Failures," this work of a loss orientation should oscillate (alternate) with a restoration orientation. But anticipatory processing does not occur if we are forewarned but are in a state of denial and/or we simply avoid thinking about the inevitable event.[9]

This period of emotional preparation between the realization that the loss will occur and when the loss actually occurs is a period of anticipatory processing. *Anticipatory processing* involves the process of mourning, coping, and psychosocial reorganization that is stimulated by the realization that the loss will occur—the project will fail. Anticipation is important in the story of Donna Heckler.

❁

In 1996, Donna started a brand strategy consulting firm. The firm offered brand strategy for clients and put brand managers on site to manage orphan brands. Over six years, she built revenues to several million dollars but was unable to make the firm profitable. Finally, after six years, Donna closed the business. She reflected on the business failure:

> *"The marketing that I did, which I love, was 'dead on,' but I did not know how to run the business side of the business. I wanted to do what I loved to do. What I knew to do was to hire the marketers, but I did not know what to look for in a finance person or an HR person, so I ended up having to do all*

these pieces. So as I think about it, the work product that we delivered was fabulous, but the business model was probably wrong, and how we went about executing the business model was wrong.

"You know, they say that creating a business is a lot like giving birth. I tell you it really was. The identity of the company was totally my identity—good or bad. The truly horrible part was before we made the decision to close the business. Before closing, I felt like I had not lived up to my potential. I had not lived up to the expectations of those working for me. I made sure to find them all other jobs, but there was an enormous feeling of guilt. I thought I was much better than that. The business was better than that.

[For Donna, the emotional reaction on the day of closing down the business was] … "relief—the hard part was making the decision that this is what I needed to do. I was taking money out of my home and making sure I was paying salaries. We never missed a paycheck, but it was such a financial burden to make sure we were taking care of everybody correctly. So by the time that I had made the decision to close the business, I felt such a relief. I should have closed the business down earlier."

Donna was aware that her business's poor performance was terminal and that failure was only a matter of time. The period of anticipatory processing (between the realization that the business will fail and when it actually does fail) gave Donna time to emotionally prepare for the failure. That is, she used this time to gradually withdraw energy from the business. This provided an emotional safeguard for when the failure eventually occurred, because the emotional bonds to the business had already been weakened.

By breaking these emotional bonds to the business, Donna could make sense of the loss, because it was seen as part of a predicted process. Decreasing the surprise of the failure event reduced the negative emotional reaction to the failure. Indeed, Donna felt relief. She was in a better position to learn from the experience and reinvest her emotions in subsequent endeavors. What is remarkable about Donna is that she was emotionally well prepared when the failure came. She accepted the loss of the business. She realized the business would fail, and she used the time before she did eventually pull the plug to emotionally prepare for its failure.

Ron Wilen, owner of a now-defunct chain of clothing stores in Pittsburgh, also found benefit in a period of emotional preparation. He concluded that separating your personal identity from the identity of the business is difficult but of critical importance. To achieve this separation, Ron acknowledged that the business was something he loved, but it was not who he was. He made attempts to step outside the business and talk to other people to help build an identity that was distinct from his business. Without achieving this separation, Ron believed that when the company died, his sense of self-worth would have been destroyed.[10]

Although anticipatory processing can reduce post-failure emotional pain, this emotional preparation comes at a cost. The emotional preparation for the transition from having the project to its being "lost" can be arduous and emotionally draining because of the conflicting demands on us. We simultaneously feel like holding onto, and letting go of, the failing project—drawing closer to it and moving away from it. For example, on the one hand, to emotionally prepare for the business's failure, Donna may have distanced herself from the business and began to separate her self-identity that was tied to the business by emphasizing membership in other groups, such as her family.[11] On the other hand, she also likely became more involved with the failing business to resolve remaining issues and "put out the many fires" that ignited as the business dropped below performance expectations. These tasks might have included trying to meet payroll, addressing customer complaints, meeting bankers to ask for an extension of an overdraft, and meeting with key suppliers to extend accounts payable to improve cash flow. These contradictory

We simultaneously feel like holding onto, and letting go of, the failing project.

tasks pulled her in opposite directions. This creates emotional turmoil.

In the end, initial benefits can result from a period of anticipatory processing for emotional preparation. But as anticipatory processing continues, these benefits are outweighed by depletion of emotional resources.

Emotionally Preparing for Failure

It's unclear how many days and months of preparation for project failure are "optimal." This amount will be different for you than for others and will be different for you across different projects. However, some period of anticipatory processing provides emotional preparation that facilitates the learning process once the failure occurs. In other words, if there is a short period between the realization that failure occurs and the failure event, you have insufficient time for any anticipatory processing to emotionally prepare for the event.

For example, a ventilated footwear project appeared highly promising. Initial tests showed that the ventilation technology lowered the foot's temperature by 7 degrees Fahrenheit and reduced the humidity within the shoe (for an overall reduction in the heat index of 42 degrees Fahrenheit). Users said they "could really feel this thing working." Then, as the tests moved to endurance testing, the technology failed, so the project was immediately terminated. The project manager, Kerrie, and the team members had very little time to prepare for the failure of this project that was so important to them. As a result, they experienced high post-failure emotional pain.

These strong emotions represent an obstacle to personally growing from the failure experience. Learning is an important aspect of personal growth, particularly when it provides us knowledge that is useful in enhancing performance in subsequent projects. For example, a manager can gain a deeper understanding of the "real" value of new opportunities, speed up the creation process, and improve performance.[12] This deeper understanding allows the manager to become more thoughtful. He or she can think along new lines, think in new patterns, and get better at searching for, and evaluating, opportunities.[13] For example, this may involve an initial screen of durability earlier in the new product development process for footwear.

❁

Learning from failure is difficult when we are experiencing emotional hurt. A learning approach—such as the oscillation model—can enhance the learning process by more effectively regulating emotions and more quickly eliminating the emotional interference. While we experience symptoms of loss, such as despair, anxiety, and anger, it is difficult for us to focus attention, energy, and emotional commitment on a subsequent project. The stronger the emotions, the more difficult, and the slower, the process of personally growing from the failure experience. As project manager of the failed "ventilated shoe," Kerrie felt bad, and therefore she found it difficult to think about the events leading up to the failure without getting upset. She took a long time to recover from the project failure, and she learned little from the experience. She was less willing to make the same sort of emotional commitment to subsequent projects, because she just did not feel she had the emotional resources to make such an investment. She had not "grown" as a result of the experience.

The emotions generated from failure, while present, reduce our ability to learn from the event and reduce our motivation to try again. The greater the post-failure reaction, the greater the emotional cost. A period of anticipatory processing (not too short or too long) reduces post-failure emotions and therefore reduces the emotional cost of failure. Thus, a period of anticipatory processing enhances the emotional preparation necessary to maximize learning from failure and provides the motivation to try again. A period of anticipatory processing represents delaying the project's termination and is in direct contrast to the economic approach of terminating the project as soon as you become aware that failure is inevitable.

> *The emotions generated from failure reduce our ability to learn from the event and reduce our motivation to try again.*

However, this is consistent with considerable evidence on how people really do make decisions.

Perhaps if the termination of the ventilated shoe project had been delayed for a week or two after the poor durability results, the project manager and the rest of the team would have been able to use this time to emotionally prepare for the failure, decreasing the level of post-failure emotions, enhancing learning from the failure experience, and maintaining the motivation to try again. Although the financial cost to the shoe company (and the manager) would have been greater, the upside is that the likelihood of success with subsequent projects would have been enhanced (from more rapid learning and greater commitment).

Balancing the Financial and Emotional Costs of Failure

When we move beyond considering just the financial costs of failure and the financial recovery for subsequent action, we realize that we must also consider the emotional costs of failure and the importance of emotional recovery to be successful with subsequent projects. We must balance the financial and emotional costs of failure to optimize personal growth. Although this balance will be different for you than for others and will be different for you for different projects, it is important to recognize that some delay in failure provides benefits. Suggesting that delay has some benefits challenges the common wisdom based on an economic rule of thumb. Although Jeff Schwartz is correct when he does the math and realizes he lost an extra $100,000 by delaying the decision to pull the plug, there was likely an emotional benefit in having done so. His emotional health is superior to what it would have been had he pulled the plug earlier. He can emotionally recover more quickly. He can learn from the experience more quickly. He may regain the motivation to "try again" more quickly. Jeff Schwartz paid $100,000 for his period of emotional preparation. Was it worth it?

The economic rule of thumb is focused on the financial costs of failure. If it is concerned only with the financial costs of failure, a project should be terminated as soon as people realize that performance is failing. This minimizes financial costs. But this provides little, or no, period of anticipatory processing. We have not had time to emotionally prepare for the loss—the emotional cost is high. As a result, it takes longer for those involved to emotionally recover from the failure event. When we delay failure, the emotional costs of failure are diminished, and personal growth is enhanced, even though this delay has a financial cost. We must be aware of this trade-off and find our optimal "balance" of financial and emotional costs for a given failing project. Maybe Jeff's personal growth from the failure experience would have benefited more from less emotional preparation and therefore would have resulted in less financial loss—say, $50,000. While we do not know the exact number, we do know that if there had been no emotional preparation ($0 extra dollars), Jeff would have suffered a high negative emotional reaction that would have made his life miserable and interfered with his ability to learn. He would have been very unlikely to try another entrepreneurial endeavor.

What Is Your Balance?

Using this anticipatory processing perspective to delay failure and persist with a project suggests the need to balance our financial and emotional costs to optimize personal growth. This balance is likely different for you than for other people and also is different for you depending on the type of project. Earlier I made the case that there are negative financial consequences to an individual's personal wealth when a project fails. However, some individuals may have much of their personal wealth insulated from failure. For example, the individual may have a diversified personal investment portfolio or has not offered personal guarantees for business loans. Or maybe failure is a badge of honor in the individual's organization. This would lower the financial cost of failure if it were to occur without any delay. If Jeff Schwartz is a very wealthy man, the "cost" to him of "financing" the emotional preparation by delaying the decision to pull the plug may well have been worth it—or at least it would not have been as devastating as it was.

However, regardless of the initial (without delay) financial cost of failure, there are likely to be differences in the rates at which financial costs are accumulated with increasing delay of the failure event. That is, the financial cost of delay is likely greater for some projects than others. For example, for projects that have a higher burn rate (higher expenditure of cash), greater financial investments are required to delay project failure. Maybe Jeff's Remarkable Memories business was burning through $10,000 a day. If so, the $100,000 bought him only ten days of emotional preparation. Another failing business might be burning through $5,000 a day. Therefore, the same emotional preparation "cost" only half as much.

Although some delay in project failure can decrease the emotions triggered by failure, we differ in our effectiveness at using this period for anticipatory processing. Some individuals may delay business failure because of an escalation of commitment or because of procrastination that keeps them in denial over the impending failure—there is little to no anticipatory processing. Therefore, this delay does not provide emotional preparation, does not weaken the emotional reaction once failure occurs, and does not enhance personal growth from failure. For example, perhaps Jeff used the information to emotionally prepare for the failure but his second partner, Sebastian, ignored the information and was in denial. The delay helped Jeff grow from the failure experience, but not Sebastian. Sebastian had not done the work necessary to begin processing the losses that had occurred and those that were about to occur. Sebastian would experience stronger emotions, learn less from the experience, and be less motivated to try again than would Jeff.

Some people may use a delay for anticipatory processing but are not good at the process. For example, in Chapter 2 you explored how learning from project failure can be enhanced when you oscillate between a loss and a restoration orientation. By improving the effectiveness of your anticipatory processing, you can achieve the emotional preparation for the loss more quickly, which reduces the financial cost for a given level of emotional recovery.

Perhaps Jeff's third partner, Beth, used the period prior to the business's failure to work through the losses that had occurred and were about to occur, but her strategy for dealing with failure (and its reaction) was not as effective as that used by Jeff. Beth continuously used a loss-orientated strategy in which she tried to work through the failure by talking about the events leading up to the business's poor performance. But invariably these discussions would turn to the emotional aspects associated with the business's decline and an anticipation of the emotions when the business would fail. These discussions caused Beth great distress, but she persisted with them and was emotionally exhausted when the business failed. Beth experienced considerable grief and little learning, and she had an aversion toward any future projects.

✷

Practical Implications

The notion of anticipatory processing and the need for some delay of the decision to terminate a project have a number of practical implications:

- Avoid delaying failure through denial, justifying past decisions to yourself or others, considering sunk costs and future investments, and generalizing the "don't waste" rule.

- Do not avoid negative emotions by delaying failure, because this will only make recovery from failure more difficult and more costly when it eventually occurs. That is, do not procrastinate.

- Recognize that delaying failure has a cost.

- When forewarned of the upcoming failure, use this time to emotionally prepare for the failure. Use the oscillation model (going back and forth from "working through" to "restoration") to process losses that have already occurred and those that are currently occurring as a result of the project's failing state.

- Think beyond this specific project to action as a series of projects across which learning can take place. That is, shift emphasis from persistence with a losing course of action with the current project to learning to find or create an eventual winning course of action across a number of future projects.

- Recognize that emotional recovery is important for subsequent success (and personal growth) because it helps you learn from the failure experience and build the motivation to try again.
- Consider the financial and emotional trade-offs when deciding to delay failure.
- As a manager of projects, forewarn project team members before the project is terminated to give them some time to emotionally prepare for its death.

Conclusion

Why do people delay failure when it is costly to do so? Sometimes it is because they are biased in their decision-making—they are wrong to do so. But some delay provides benefits. People experience emotions over failure (to a greater or lesser degree). These negative emotions retard learning and retard the building of the motivation to try again. Some delay provides the opportunity for anticipatory processing. Anticipatory processing is stimulated by a forewarning of the loss of the project. It involves an awareness of the losses that have already occurred or are occurring now as a result of the project's failing

Personal growth is optimized by balancing the financial and emotional costs of failure.

state. It reduces the emotional reaction to the failure event. Thus, anticipatory processing enhances emotional preparation and learning from failure. That is, we can engage in subsequent projects with increased odds of success. Personal growth is optimized by balancing the financial and emotional costs of failure. Some delay of failure helps achieve this balance.

❋

Endnotes

[1] Useem, J. (1998). "Failure: The Secret of My Success." *Inc.* http://www.inc.com/magazine/19980501/922.html.

[2] Shepherd, D.A. Wiklund, J., and Haynie, J.M. (2008). "Moving forward: Balancing the financial and emotional costs of business failure." *Journal of Business Venturing*, 24: 134–148.

[3] Karlsson, N., Juliusson, E.A., and Gärling, T. (2005). "A conceptualization of task dimensions affecting escalation of commitment." *European Journal of Cognitive Psychology*, 17: 835–858.

[4] Cooper, A.C., Woo, C.A., and Dunkelberg, W. (1988). "Entrepreneurs perceived chances for success." *Journal of Business Venturing*, 3: 97–108.

[5] Arkes, H.R. and Blumer, C. (1985). "The psychology of sunk loss." *Organizational Behavior and Human Decision Processes*, 35: 124–140.

[6] Schmidt, J. and Calantone, R. (2002). "Escalation of commitment during new product development." *Academy of Marketing Science Journal*, 30(2): 103–129.

7   Tversky, A. and Kahneman, D. (1981). "The framing of decisions and the psychology of choice." *Science*, 211: 453–458.

8   Van Eerde, W. (2000). "Procrastination: Self-regulation in initiating aversive goals." *Applied Psychology: An International Review*, 49: 372–389.

9   Kübler-Ross, E. (1969). *On Death and Dying*. New York: Springer.

10 Useem, J. (1998).

11 Major, B. and Schmader, T. (1998). "Coping with stigma through psychological disengagement." In J.K. Swim and C. Stangor (eds.), *Prejudice: The Target's Perspective*, pp. 219–41. San Diego, CA: Academic.

12 Davidsson, P. and Honig, B. (2003). "The role of social and human capital among nascent owner-managers." *Journal of Business Venturing*, 18(3): 301–332.

13 Rerup, C. (2005). "Learning from past experience: Footnotes on mindfulness and habitual entrepreneurship." *Scandinavian Journal of Management*, 21: 451–472.

"IF YOU WANT OTHERS TO BE HAPPY,
PRACTICE COMPASSION. IF YOU WANT
TO BE HAPPY, PRACTICE COMPASSION."
—THE DALAI LAMA

"EVERY ACT OF CONSCIOUS LEARNING
REQUIRES THE WILLINGNESS TO SUFFER
AN INJURY TO ONE'S SELF-ESTEEM.
THAT IS WHY YOUNG CHILDREN,
BEFORE THEY ARE AWARE OF THEIR
OWN SELF-IMPORTANCE, LEARN SO
EASILY; AND WHY OLDER PERSONS,
ESPECIALLY IF VAIN OR IMPORTANT,
CANNOT LEARN AT ALL."
—THOMAS SZASZ

CHAPTER 4

SELF-COMPASSION TO LEARN FROM FAILURE

When we have lost something that is important to us, it is natural to feel bad. It is what we do about these emotions that is the key to our ability to learn from the failure experience. Before discussing self-compassion, it is important to detail the more common strategies for dealing with project failure. These common strategies are used to make us feel good about our abilities and self-worth, but they are also the very strategies that stop us from learning what would really help us improve ourselves. Indeed, by using strategies to protect our positive self views after project failure, we contribute to a higher likelihood that we will make the same mistakes again. For example, you could blame the project failure on bad luck. This helps you feel good about yourself but does not direct your attention toward collecting and processing information that will help you learn from the mistake and avoid it in the future. Then why do we pursue these strategies?

The negative emotional reaction to project failure necessitates a response. Without a response, these emotions persist, and perhaps increase through ruminations, which can have consequences. We act to maintain a healthy well-being, and central to that is our self-esteem. Your self-esteem is your overall appraisal of self-worth. Indeed, one of our most fundamental assumptions is to believe the self worthy.[1]

The failure of a project that is important to you generates negative emotions, but it also often represents an event that has the potential to "hit" your self-esteem. Failure has the potential to make you feel less capable. Big failures have the potential to be traumatic and shatter the fundamental assumption that the self is worthy. I say "potential" because we are very effective at enacting mechanisms that protect the ego (self-esteem) from these attacks. But as you will see, these ego-protective strategies obstruct learning.

✷

As the national HR manager for freight company DHL Express, Nicky Harrison recognizes the importance of experimentation and learning from failure and how this process can be obstructed when people feel the need to protect themselves from blame: "If a blame culture is allowed to pervade an organization, people don't feel able to stretch and make their own decisions about what is best for the customer, which is what DHL Express wants its people to have the freedom to do. We encourage our staff to think outside the square—inevitably there will be some failings, but it's possible to learn from these and fold that learning back into [the job]."[2]

However, learning from failure is more complicated than simply working in an organizational culture that understands that failure happens and that it is an opportunity to learn. For example, Henry was second in charge of the Pool Be Clean team that attempted to develop and exploit a self-cleaning pool filter, but the project was terminated by top management after six months of development efforts. Henry was devastated by the failure. Because he had invested so much of his time and effort and had so much of his identity tied to the success of the project, he felt the failure represented a personal threat. He started questioning himself about whether he really was a worthwhile individual. Rather than head down this

Learning from failure is more complicated than simply working in an organizational culture that understands that failure happens and that it is an opportunity to learn.

path and start thinking less of himself, he started to think in ways that made him feel better about himself. He convinced himself that he was not to blame for the design of the valve that kept failing in durability tests. It was the fault of the suppliers of the source materials. It was the fault of the "users," who were too rough on the equipment. It was the fault of top management for not having enough entrepreneurial spirit to take the risk and launch the product now and work out the kinks later. He began to feel better about the failure, because what could he do?—it wasn't his fault.

He also started thinking about Larry, the project leader of the "hands-free underwater vacuum cleaner." It had allowed battery chemicals to leak into the pool, causing serious illness to 150 customers. The failure of his own project was much smaller than that. When he thought about Larry, Henry felt better about himself.

One ego-protective strategy that Henry used is *downward comparison*—his comparison to poor, unfortunate Larry. Downward comparison is where we compare ourselves to others who are doing less well in order to provide or maintain positive self-esteem. When we look at our incompetence that led to project failure, we can feel better about ourselves by comparing ourselves to others who have demonstrated great incompetence, who suffered stigma from the failure, who were fired by the organization, who do not have a job, who have boring or grueling jobs. For example, Henry compares himself not only to Larry, but also to the "bean counter" in the front office, who must have the most boring job in the world. And he compares his own role to James, who has the most demanding job of digging the ditches for pool plumbing.

This downward comparison does not need to accurately reflect the others' conditions or competencies, nor does it need to be an actual person. It could be based on simply imagining a person "out there" who has these disadvantaged characteristics. Henry could imagine what it would be like to be the guy he saw on the Discovery Channel whose job it is to clean toilets at a large Indian market. In fact, Henry's favorite show is *Dirty Jobs*, where each week they show some unfortunate character who has the most unimaginably bad job. Such comparisons allow Henry to feel superior to others despite recently experiencing a failure. This allows him to keep a belief in positive self-worth despite evidence that he had made some serious mistakes in the Pool Be Clean project.

Rather than accept our contribution to the failure and our current situation, we often use an alternative ego-protective strategy called an *attribution bias*. An attribution bias reflects our tendency to attribute good outcomes to our own skills, knowledge, and/or experience and attribute poor outcomes, such as failure, to others' actions and/or environmental conditions beyond our control. That is, we are responsible for our successes but not for our failures. In using this strategy, the success (whether actually due to our actions or things beyond our control) is used to build positive self-esteem; this approach also helps us maintain positive self-esteem in the face of project failure. In essence, this ego-protective strategy protects the self from negative feedback about our incompetence. Henry also used this strategy. By blaming others for the failure, he was able to feel better about himself.

Whether using downward comparison or an attribution bias, we protect our self-esteem. Maintaining high self-esteem has a number of advantages. By using these ego-protective strategies, Henry maintained high motivation to achieve success with the next project. Higher motivation can provide a number of positive performance implications—the more motivated you are, the higher your performance on tasks (holding all else constant). If Henry had not used these ego-protective strategies and allowed his belief in self-worth to drop, he would have been less motivated, would have performed less well on subsequent projects, would have had higher levels of dissatisfaction with work and life, and would have been more likely to have physical and psychological problems.[3]

These represent some pretty good reasons for pursuing ego-protective strategies—strategies that we have become very good at engaging and enacting. But they do come at a cost.

The use of ego-protective strategies, not surprisingly, leads to an overemphasis on liking oneself. While we all should hopefully like ourselves, because we have to live in our own skin and live our own life, over-liking oneself is taking this a step further and has been associated with narcissism, self-absorption, and self-centeredness.[4] Most of us can think of someone we know who thinks this way and, thus, why it is not always positive. You need to be aware that your ego-protective strategies can take you down this road. For example, take the downward comparison strategy: When accurate, downward comparisons focus our attention on people's weaknesses and/or their disadvantaged positions. Often our downward comparisons are based on assumptions about others—we assume the worst in others as a means of rating ourselves higher by comparison.[5]

When Henry used these mental strategies to feel better about himself in the face of the project failure, he was disconnecting himself further from the project and, thus, further from the chance to learn from the project. That is, these ego-protective strategies erect substantial barriers to learning. Downward comparisons lower the bar for our expected performance to make us feel better about ourselves. But it is the gap between our aspiration level and our actual performance level that provides the motivation to learn. The more Henry compares himself to people like Larry, the lower the bar is set for expected performance. By

> *When there is a gap, or disconnect, which you feel as an emotional reaction, you are motivated to close the gap by raising your performance to that of the standard.*

exceeding this lower bar for performance, Henry can keep feeling good about himself, but there is less incentive to improve on his current performance. When there is a gap, or disconnect, which you feel as an emotional reaction, you are motivated to close the gap by raising your performance to that of the standard. The gap, and the emotions that we feel as a result of the gap, stimulates us to focus attention on scanning for new information about why the project failed, use our cognitive resources to process the newly scanned information, and learn to develop a plausible story for the project's failure. Henry used downward comparisons to close the gap by lowering performance expectations, thereby circumventing the urgency to make sense of the project's failure.

Similarly, the ego-protective strategy of an attribution bias obstructs learning from failure. To the extent you attribute the cause of the failure to others and environments beyond your control, you tell yourself there is nothing to learn. What can you learn that enables you to decrease the likelihood of similar mistakes when you believe (perhaps falsely) that you cannot influence the source of these failures? The more Henry believes that the failure was someone else's fault, the less there is for him to learn. He can't control the behaviors of others.

Although this attribution bias can help protect the ego, it can also undermine it, because it reinforces the notion that we do not have control over our own destiny. Even for the projects we care deeply about, the sources of the project failure can occur repeatedly. They can lead to learned helplessness and a reduction in self-esteem and motivation. Although, again, we are good at self-delusion, attributing past project failures to external factors and attributing the success of future projects to our own actions.

Two Project Team Leaders with Self-Compassion

Take two development teams dealing with the failure of their projects (loosely based on true projects). The first project, Pool Be Clean, was a self-cleaning pool filter that required less work by the pool owner and wasted less water. However, the large valve necessary to "flip" and "burp" out the leaves and dirty water had only a short life and could not be cost effectively lengthened. The project was terminated by the organization's top management. The project leader, Holly, second-in-charge Henry, and the rest of the team had invested a lot of time, effort, and creativity into this project and felt awful after its termination.

The second project team, Dolphin Away, was developing a miniaturized version of a sonar device to put on fishing nets to keep dolphins out of the nets and save their lives. However, the sonar frequency kept away only specific species of dolphins. It was believed that the sonar frequency may attract sharks, causing them to be caught in the nets and resulting in extensive damage to the nets. The project was terminated by top management. Isabel, the team leader, as well as Emily, the chief researcher, were dedicated to the project and to saving dolphins, and they both felt awful over the project's failure.

Overall, ego-protective strategies, including downward comparisons and attribution bias, are often effective at maintaining motivation after project failure for investment in a subsequent project, but they also obstruct your ability to learn from the failure experience. We are likely doomed to make the same mistakes again. Henry, from Pool Be Clean, attributed the possibility of project success to his own actions right up until that project failed. At that point, he rationalized that, all along, it was beyond his control and was caused by those beyond his control.

Self-compassion represents a superior alternative to ego-protective strategies.

Emily, from Dolphin Away, poses a contrast to Henry. She had self-compassion. She was touched by her emotional pain over the project failure. She focused on engaging her feelings and emotions to personally grow from the experience rather than engage in strategies to disconnect from the project failure to maintain a positive view of herself. By engaging and exploring her emotions generated from project failure (rather than trying to avoid them), Emily had the opportunity to more freely explore the causes of the project's failure and maintain a high performance threshold. Self-compassion represents a superior alternative to ego-protective strategies; it does not involve a trade-off between learning from failure and the motivation to try again.

Self-Compassion and Failure

Self-compassion provides caring and compassion toward oneself in the face of hardship. It is this caring and compassion that provide a buffer against the anxiety that failure creates through its threat to the ego. In one laboratory study, when facing a potential ego-threatening situation, those with high self-compassion felt better about themselves, their work, and their lives than those who had less self-compassion.

Project failure leads to negative emotions—the more important the project, the worse we feel. These emotions interfere with our ability to learn from our failure experiences. As mentioned, project failure can activate ego-protective mechanisms that, while weakening our emotional reaction, obstruct learning from failure. Self-compassion—kindness, common humanity, and mindfulness—can be activated by project failure, diminishing the activation and use of ego-protective strategies. Self-compassion does not directly influence the emotions we feel over project failure, but it helps reduce the negative effect that these emotions have on learning and maximizes its learning benefits.

Individuals who are self-kind in assessing failure (self-kindness), who place failure in perspective with others (common humanity), and who have their emotions in balance (mindfulness) are better able to learn from the experience and are motivated to apply the new knowledge in subsequent projects.[6] They are better able to personally grow from their failure experiences.

How self-compassionate are you?

How self-compassionate are you? Respond to the surveys in Tables 4.1, 4.2, and 4.3. In Table 4.1, circle the number that best represents how often you act in the stated manner for each of the ten statements, where 1 is almost never and 5 is almost always. Add up your score for the self-kindness subscale (your score will be between 5 and 25). Do the same for the self-judgment subscale. Subtract the self-judgment score from the self-kindness score. This is your overall self-kindness score. Repeat the same process for Table 4.2 for your overall common humanity score. Repeat the process again for Table 4.3 for your overall mindfulness score. To compare your scores against a benchmark, in a study of undergraduate students from a large Southwestern university in the U.S., the average overall score for self-kindness was −0.5 (15.3 for self-kindness and 15.8 for self-judgment). For common humanity it was 0.0 (12.0 for common humanity and 12.0 for isolation). For mindfulness it was 1.4 (13.6 for mindfulness and 12.2 for overidentification). Figure 4.1 shows the total scores for each dimension of self-compassion, as well as the scores for Emily and

Henry (discussed in the next section). Plot your score to see how you measure up. If you have a low score, the important lesson is that you need to show yourself more compassion. Otherwise, you are erecting barriers to your ability to learn from failure and grow from the experience. I detail at the end of the chapter how you can achieve this.

Table 4.1 Are You More Self-Kind or More Self-Judgmental?

Indicate how often you act in the manner stated:

Almost Never			Almost Always	
1	2	3	4	5

Self-Kindness Subscale

I try to be understanding and patient toward those aspects of my personality I don't like	1 2 3 4 5
I'm kind to myself when I'm experiencing suffering	1 2 3 4 5
When I'm going through a very hard time, I give myself the caring and tenderness I need	1 2 3 4 5
I'm tolerant of my own flaws and inadequacies	1 2 3 4 5
I try to be loving toward myself when I'm feeling emotional pain	1 2 3 4 5

Self-Judgment Subscale

When I see aspects of myself that I don't like, I get down on myself	1 2 3 4 5
When times are really difficult, I tend to be tough on myself	1 2 3 4 5
I can be a bit coldhearted toward myself when I'm experiencing suffering	1 2 3 4 5
I'm disapproving and judgmental about my own flaws and inadequacies	1 2 3 4 5
I'm intolerant and impatient toward those aspects of my personality I don't like	1 2 3 4 5

Scale is from Neff.[7]

If you score higher on the self-kindness subscale than on the self-judgment subscale, you are more self-kind than self-judgmental. The opposite is true if you scored higher on the self-judgment subscale.

Table 4.2 Do You Feel Part of Common Humanity or Isolated?

Indicate how often you act in the manner stated:

Almost Never			Almost Always	
1	2	3	4	5

Common Humanity Subscale

When I feel inadequate in some way, I try to remind myself that feelings of inadequacy are shared by most people	1 2 3 4 5
I try to see my failings as part of the human condition	1 2 3 4 5
When I'm down and out, I remind myself that there are other people in the world feeling like I am	1 2 3 4 5
When things are going bad for me, I see the difficulties as part of life that everyone goes through	1 2 3 4 5

Isolation Subscale

When I fail at something that's important to me, I tend to feel alone in my failure	1 2 3 4 5
When I think about my inadequacies, it tends to make me feel more separate and cut off from the rest of the world	1 2 3 4 5
When I'm feeling down, I tend to feel like most other people are probably happier than I am	1 2 3 4 5
When I'm really struggling, I tend to feel like other people must be having an easier time of it	1 2 3 4 5

Scale is from Neff.[8]

If you score higher on the common humanity subscale than on the isolation subscale, you are more associated with common humanity than with isolation. The opposite is true if you scored higher on the isolation subscale.

Table 4.3 Are You More Mindful or Overidentified?

Indicate how often you act in the manner stated:

Almost Never			Almost Always	
1	2	3	4	5

Mindfulness Subscale

When something upsets me, I try to keep my emotions in balance	1 2 3 4 5
When I'm feeling down, I try to take a balanced view of the situation	1 2 3 4 5
When something painful happens, I try to take a balanced view of the situation	1 2 3 4 5
When I fail at something important to me, I try to keep things in perspective	1 2 3 4 5

Overidentification Subscale

When something upsets me, I get carried away with my feelings	1 2 3 4 5
When I'm feeling down, I tend to obsess and fixate on everything that's wrong	1 2 3 4 5
When something painful happens, I tend to blow the incident out of proportion	1 2 3 4 5
When I fail at something important to me, I become consumed by feelings of inadequacy	1 2 3 4 5

Scale is from Neff.[9]

If you score higher on the mindfulness subscale than on the overidentification subscale, you are more mindful than overidentifying. The opposite is true if you scored higher on the overidentification subscale.

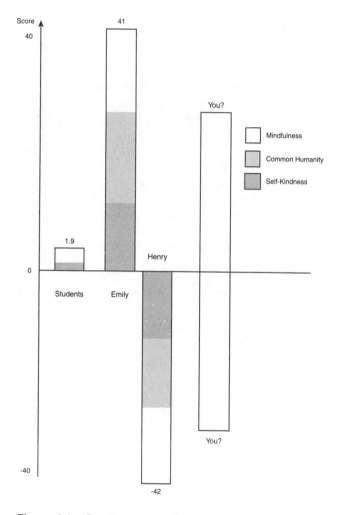

Figure 4.1 Chart your score for project importance

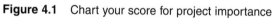

Self-Kindness and Failure

If you scored high on the self-kindness subscale of Table 4.1 (total score above 0), you show self-kindness. When it comes to project failure, *self-kindness* refers to extending kindness and understanding to yourself. Contrast this with people who, upon making a mistake that leads to project failure, engage in self-criticism. Although judgment and criticism can be a source of feedback for learning, their harsh and critical tone means that they are likely to lead to a lowering of self-esteem or the activation of ego-protective strategies. For example, whether he is playing tennis, fishing, or at work, when something goes wrong, Henry slaps his leg, starts hitting his forehead, and berates himself for making such a "stupid mistake," for being "such an idiot," and for overlooking such an "obvious signal." This harsh, critical tone quickly triggers the use of the ego-protective mechanisms such as "The ball is flat," "Larry would not even have hooked the fish in the first place," and "The customers must be crazy for using the pool filter in that way." Henry is highly self-critical. On the self-kindness subscale of Table 4.1, his total score is −13 (his score for self-kindness was 8 and for self-judgment was 21), as shown in Figure 4.1.

Self-kindness leads us down an alternative path. First, self-kindness provides a self-created environment that affords you the opportunity to gain a deeper understanding of the negative aspects of yourself. By extending kindness and caring to ourselves, we can explore our personal attributes or actions that may have contributed to the project's failing. We can do so in a way that does not threaten the ego. We want to find out what we did wrong, not to harshly criticize ourselves such that our mistakes are interpreted as an overall negative evaluation of us as a person. While our actions may have been wrong, when displaying self-kindness, this determination is not generalized to us as people overall. For example, Emily can more objectively look at her own mistakes because she is kind and caring to herself. She gives herself a break by not being overly hard on herself for her mistakes. While she acknowledges that she did make a mistake, it does not mean that she is stupid, bad, or an idiot. Emily's total score on the self-kindness subscale was 10 (22 for self-kindness and 12 for self-judgment), as shown in Figure 4.1.

Second, being kind to yourself acknowledges that the emotions you feel over project failure can be intense and can hurt. Those who are self-kind realize that they are feeling emotional pain and take actions to ease that pain, or at least not exacerbate it. For example, Emily takes a break from emotionally draining tasks by doing something nice. When a project fails, she treats herself to a favorite restaurant, a ball game, or a musical. She is not rewarding herself for contributing to failure, but simply showing self-kindness during an emotionally difficult time.

Third, and related to the preceding point, self-kindness means that we are caring toward ourselves as we go through hard times. For example, as she goes through a tough patch at work with the failure of Dolphin Away, Emily takes some of the other pressures off by, for example, putting off the do-it-yourself tiling of her bathroom, canceling the visit to her in-laws, or rescheduling the parent-teacher conference.

Finally, those who are self-kind are more tolerant of their own flaws and inadequacies. This is especially important when those flaws and inadequacies contributed to the project failure. For example, I know that one of my flaws is that in a rush to get things done, I sometimes make mistakes. If I had taken more time writing a manuscript, perhaps it would not need so many changes. I realize that I need more speed and less haste, and I do not "beat myself up" over this issue. I accept the flaw, and I work on overcoming it.

❁

By extending our kindness, we are less harsh in our self-criticism—the type of negative feedback that is often seen as a threat to the ego, stimulating ego-protective mechanisms that obstruct learning. Self-kindness allows us to stay connected to the failure in a way that enhances learning. Importantly, self-kindness is within our grasp. We already extend kindness to friends, family members, and colleagues. When

We're often kind to others who fail but overly harsh on ourselves.

showing kindness to a friend who contributed to a project's failing, what would you say? Why? You obviously think that it helps him or her deal with the situation. You give him or her a break. Why not extend yourself the same courtesy? We're often kind to others who fail but overly harsh on ourselves.

Being self-kind does not mean that you are giving yourself a free pass. It does not mean you are ignoring your contribution to the failure or passively accepting that contribution. The opposite is the case. Self-kindness removes the type of harsh self-criticism that results in the erection of ego-protective barriers, such as Henry's harshly critical self-talk that triggered the use of downward comparisons and the attribution of blame to other people and things beyond his control. Henry used these ego-protective strategies to screen out inadequacy from self-awareness, but these strategies obstructed learning. They stopped Henry from learning more about why the Pool Be Clean project failed and stopped him from learning more about himself—what he knows, what he does not know, what emotions he feels, how to control those emotions, and so on.

Self-kindness provides an emotional safety net (of awareness of your mistakes without harsh criticism for making those mistakes) to provide an objective perspective of the failure event. Therefore, self-kindness helps prevent thoughts about the event from settling on negative emotions and threatening your fundamental beliefs about being a worthwhile person. Awareness of your mistakes and weaknesses is important for learning from failure. Self-kindness helps build this awareness.

More importantly, self-kindness does not diminish the emotional importance of the project that failed. It does not weaken our emotional reaction. But it does require that you not judge yourself as a bad person even though you made a serious mistake. Doing so requires *discriminating wisdom*. Discriminating wisdom allows you to evaluate your mistakes, errors, and lapses in judgment, but to do so with compassion—a compassionate understanding of the context in which the failure took place and that the context is often complex and dynamic. This is not blaming the failure on these external conditions of uncertainty and/or time pressures. Instead, it provides a more caring basis upon which to understand your contribution to the failure. And these mistakes are not taken as indicators of self-worth.[10] That is, self-kindness allows you to divorce the causes of failure from the global evaluations of yourself, thereby erecting fewer obstacles to learning. Both Henry and Emily were equally committed to their respective projects. They both felt bad when it failed. But Emily understands that these new projects involve uncertainty and time pressure and that, in these environments, mistakes happen. Her self-kindness allows her to explore her mistakes and weaknesses without threatening her self-beliefs.

Common Humanity and Failure

The second dimension of self-compassion is *common humanity*. If you scored high on the common humanity subscale of Table 4.2 (total score above 0), you put your failures and yourself in the perspective of others rather than cut yourself off from the experiences of other people. Compare yourself to Emily and Henry. Which one are you more like? Emily's total score for the common humanity subscale of Table 4.2 is 15 (22 for common humanity and 7 for isolation), and Henry's total score for the common humanity subscale is −13 (6 for common humanity and 19 for isolation), as shown in Figure 4.1.

First, we exhibit common humanity when we remind ourselves that our feelings of personal doubt are shared by most people who experience failure. For example, Emily reminds herself when a project fails that her feelings of inadequacy are normal. Most people have a negative emotional reaction to the failure of their project, especially if that project was important to them, and they feel a little insecure about their ability to be successful in the future. But Emily was able to say to herself that "All people feel this sadness I feel when a project fails" and "Others can cope with these feelings; so can I." She can take some comfort in that "Those who have felt this bad in the past eventually feel better" and that some people "feel they are a better person as a result of the experience." This enables her to keep her emotions and feelings of vulnerability in check.

Henry, in contrast, becomes self-critical even of his emotional reaction to the failure: "You feel sad; you're such a baby," "I'm the only emotional mess in this whole organization," "Why am I so weak?" Henry starts feeling bad not only about the mistakes that led to the project's failure but also about his emotional reaction to the failure, which compounds the problem to make him feel even worse.

Second, showing common humanity recognizes that the project failure was caused by our personal mistakes and weaknesses. But it puts those mistakes and weaknesses in context by acknowledging that all people have weaknesses and all people make mistakes sometimes. For example, Emily reminds herself that most people experience a failure of some sort during their working lives, especially those working on new projects. By putting it in this perspective, Emily triggers a caring and compassion attitude toward herself in the face of the Dolphins Away failure. This enables her to see the failure as not so much an indictment of her mistakes and weakness, because we all have them. On the other hand, Henry's self-judgmental approach focuses on his mistakes and weaknesses and highlight how different he is from others. For example, his self-talk includes "Andrew would never make such a stupid mistake," "This mistake will go down in company history as the dumbest ever," and "Why am I the only one who makes such obvious slip-ups?" This line of thinking triggers his ego-protective strategies. For others, it might lead them to believe that they are not worthy individuals.

Finally, we show common humanity when we remind ourselves that many projects are risky. Projects often involve something new—new products, new processes, new markets. We pursue new avenues because they often represent the promise of high gains, but they exist because we, and others, are uncertain whether those benefits will material-ize. When our project pursues something new but fails, we must realize that in these highly uncertain environments, mistakes and failure are relatively common. Despite realizing that failures are relative-ly common with the sorts of projects she works on, Emily still feels bad when the project fails. But she can keep the failure and her emotions in check. She tells herself that "Hindsight is always 20/20," "It is great to look in the rearview mirror to see where you have been and perhaps what you have run over, but the future requires that we all must anticipate what is around the next bend," and "We would not make mistakes if we had all the information and ample time—but we don't." Henry scolds himself for his unique ability to miss signals about what would happen given that they are obvious to every-one now.

❂

Showing common humanity allows you to perceive your project failure as part of the larger human experience. It is put in a broader context. This broader context means that you no longer focus on your uniqueness in contributing to project failure. You no longer isolate yourself from others. Rather, you remain connected to others—you are all human after all. By taking a common humanity per-spective, Emily remained connected with others on the team and the rest of the organization. This gave her access to an additional source of information for learning from the failure. They confided to her some of their thoughts about what caused the failure and provided documentation from the engineering department about the reverberating sonar component. Remaining connected to others also helped her enact the "emotion-management" strategies and deal with a loss orientation, restoration orientation, and transition orientation.

By remaining connected with others, and after she had learned from the failure and personally grown from the experience, Emily still had a network to mobilize resources that were important for success with her next project. These benefits were unavailable to Henry, who had isolated himself from others by focusing on the uniqueness of his mistakes, the project failure, and his own attributes and flaws.

Therefore, by perceiving your failure experience in light of the common human experience, you can acknowledge that failure is a common occurrence in the business process and that all people engaged in this process—yourself included—deserve compassion when failure occurs. For example, "Realizing that suffering and personal failures are shared with others lessens the degree of blame and judgment placed on oneself."[11] Showing common humanity lessens self-blame, and it does so differently than ego-protective strategies such as externalizing blame (blaming others or conditions for the failure) and downward comparisons.

Downward comparisons involve focusing comparisons on more disadvantaged groups to maintain high self-esteem (such as Henry's focusing on poor,

Common humanity acknowledges failures in all people, including yourself.

unfortunate Larry, who seriously injured a large number of customers). Common humanity acknowledges failures in all people, including yourself. Therefore, there is less judgment of yourself, because contrasts to specific others are not possible and are not needed to defend self-esteem. They are not possible because common humanity applies to all people, not to specific individuals or specific groups. It does not highlight individuals or groups (advantaged or disadvantaged); we are all in the same boat (even Larry). Downward comparisons are not necessary because by showing common humanity, your failures are not perceived as a threat to your ego.

As with self-kindness, showing common humanity does not diminish the emotional importance of the failed project. We still feel bad. But the failure and your emotions are put in perspective, such that you can more quickly learn from the experience.

Mindfulness and Failure

The final dimension of self-compassion is *mindfulness*. Mindfulness involves holding the painful thoughts and feelings in balanced awareness rather than overidentifying with these emotions. A more mindful person achieves this "balanced awareness" by approaching his or her feelings with curiosity and openness rather than shame and close-mindedness. Being curious about and open toward our emotions has the benefit of acknowledging that our feelings contain important information. We can use our emotions to signal to us that something important has happened. This focuses our attention on scanning for information and processing that information to learn about the events surrounding the project failure that triggered our negative emotions. Curiosity and openness provide the motivation to explore our emotions and failures. They also help reduce the anxiety over how to control our emotions. Actually, they do not need to be controlled; rather, they are an important part of the process of learning from failure.

Henry was low in mindfulness. His total score for the mindfulness subscale of Table 4.3 was −16 (6 for mindfulness and 22 for overidentification), as shown in Figure 4.1. He overidentified with the emotions generated by the failure of Pool Be Clean. That is, rather than explore the underlying events that led to the failure signaled by his emotions, Henry focused on the emotions themselves. He became carried away with, wrapped

Mindfulness involves holding the painful thoughts and feelings in balanced awareness rather than overidentifying with these emotions.

up in, and completely absorbed by his own feelings.[12] We all have the potential to become self-absorbed. In Chapter 2, "Strategies to Learn More from Your Failures," I highlighted how, by pursuing a loss orientation for an extended period, our thoughts move from the events surrounding the failure to the emotions generated by the failure. We begin to ruminate. We think about how bad we feel. We think about how bad others feel as a result of the failure. And this makes us feel worse. This rumination exacerbates these emotions, further interfering with learning from failure.

This focus on the emotions of failure associated with an extended period of loss orientation is consistent with someone low in mindfulness. The longer we hold a loss orientation, the more danger there is that we have less mindfulness. Low mindfulness can result in escalating negative emotions, diminishing our ability to learn from failure.

❂

Emily is mindful. Her total score for the mindfulness subscale of Table 4.3 was 16 (20 for mindfulness and 4 for overidentification), as shown in Figure 4.1. She acknowledges feeling bad over the failure of Dolphin Away, but she can avoid the sort of severe judgment and harsh criticisms that blur the failure event and overall assessments of self-worth. In doing so, Emily eliminates the threatening nature of the project failure to her self-esteem. Therefore, that failure event does not activate ego-protective strategies that obstruct learning from failure.

Emily accepts failure as an opportunity to learn, even though it is emotionally painful. This allows the events leading up to the failure to be brought into conscious awareness (not pushed away and hidden by ego-protective strategies) so that they can be analyzed to form a plausible story about why Dolphin Away failed. This does not mean that emotions are ignored or normalized (see Chapter 6, "Preparing for Multiple Failures"). Instead, emotions are acknowledged but compartmentalized, separate from assessments of self-worth. Emotions are a source of information to be explored by a mind that is curious and open.

Failure generates the opportunity to learn and generates negative emotions. A mindful individual holds these two in balance while each is processed. Although more mindful people are better at keeping these two functions in balance, as I detailed in Chapter 2, everyone can improve their "balance" by oscillating between a loss orientation and a restoration orientation. Those who more effectively manage the oscillation orientation show greater mindfulness. It is important to note that mindfulness does not mean that the individual is detached from the learning process. Rather, he or she detaches the evaluation of the causes of the failure from evaluations of the self. Indeed, mindfulness is a situation where the sense of the self softens or disappears. This open, nonjudgmental attention stance does not threaten the ego, and therefore ego-protective strategies are not deployed. Thus, mindfulness helps avoid the erection of obstacles to learning that are often present when thinking about a failure event.

Practical Implications

- Avoid ego-protective strategies when facing failure, because they obstruct learning. Instead, show self-compassion.

- Attempt to gain a deeper understanding of the negative aspects of yourself. These may include personal attributes and/or actions that contributed to the failure.

- Be kind to yourself during the process of dealing with emotional pain and suffering. This involves doing something nice to yourself in an attempt to ease the emotional pain or at least not further contribute to it by "beating yourself up" over the failure.

- Be caring toward yourself while going through the "hard times" after failure. Realize that you are in an emotionally vulnerable state, and don't "push" emotional issues too far.

- Tolerate your own flaws and inadequacies, especially those that contributed to the failure.

- Remind yourself that feelings of inadequacy are shared by most people who experience failure.

- See your contribution to the failure as resulting from personal weaknesses and mistakes and that all people have weaknesses and all people make mistakes sometimes.

- Remind yourself that because opportunities exist in an uncertain environment, most people involved with new projects make mistakes that could lead to failure.

- Remind yourself that most people feel bad over failure, which requires a process of discovery that takes time.
- Keep the emotions generated by the failure in balance.
- Approach feelings and emotions with curiosity and openness.
- Maintain a distinction between the failure event and your self-worth.

Conclusion

When we experience failure, our natural inclination is to protect our self-esteem; we do this through ego-protective strategies. While these are often effective in protecting our feelings of self-worth, they also erect obstacles to learning from failure. An alternative way of dealing with failure and its associated emotions is to show self-compassion. By showing self-kindness, common humanity, and mindfulness, you detach your self-worth from the failure on a project, which means that ego-protective strategies are not needed. This results in fewer obstacles to failure so that you can more effectively process the events surrounding the failure to learn from the failure experience. Showing self-compassion facilitates learning from failure.

❂

Endnotes

1 Janoff-Buhlman, R. and Frieze, I.H. (1983). "A theoretical perspective for understanding reaction to victimization." *Journal of Social Issues*, 39: 1–17.

2 "Do mention the 'F' word." *New Zealand Herald*, August 12, 2006.

3 Buttner, E.H. (1992). "Entrepreneurial stress: Is it hazardous to your health?" *Journal of Managerial Issues*, 4: 223–240; Jamal, M. (1997). "Job stress, satisfaction, and mental health: An empirical examination of self-employed and non-self-employed Canadians." *Journal of Small Business Management*, 35(4): 48–57; Jamal, M. and Badawi, J.A. (1995). "Job stress and quality of working life of self-employed immigrants: A study in workforce diversity." *Journal of Small Business and Entrepreneurship*, 12: 55–63.

4 Damon, W. (1995). *Greater Expectations: Overcoming the Culture of Indulgence in America's Homes and Schools*. New York: Free Press; Ryan, R.M. and Deci, E.L. (2001). "On happiness and human potential: A review of research on hedonic and eudaemonic well-being." *Annual Review of Psychology*, 52: 141–166.

5 Crocker, J., Thompson, L.L., McGraw, K.M., and Ingerman, C. (1987). "Downward comparison, prejudice, and evaluations of others: Effects of self-esteem and threat." *Journal of Personality and Social Psychology*, 52: 907–916.

6 Shepherd, D.A. and Cardon, M. "Negative emotional reactions to project failure and the self-compassion to learn from the experience." *Journal of Management Studies* (forthcoming).

7   Neff, K.D. (2003b). "The development and validation of a scale to measure self-compassion." *Self and Identity*, 2: 223–250.

8   Ibid.

9   Ibid.

10 Neff, K.D., Hsieh, Y., and Dejitthirat, K. (2005). "Self-compassion, achievement goals, and coping with academic failure." *Self and Identity*, 4: 263–287.

11 Neff, K.D. (2003a). "Self-compassion: An alternative conceptualization of a healthy attitude toward oneself." *Self and Identity*, 2: 85–102 (page 87).

12 Ibid.

"DON'T THINK YOU CAN ATTAIN
TOTAL AWARENESS AND WHOLE
ENLIGHTENMENT WITHOUT PROPER
DISCIPLINE AND PRACTICE. THIS IS
EGOMANIA. APPROPRIATE RITUALS
CHANNEL YOUR EMOTIONS AND LIFE
ENERGY TOWARD THE LIGHT. WITHOUT
THE DISCIPLINE TO PRACTICE THEM, YOU
WILL TUMBLE CONSTANTLY BACKWARD
INTO DARKNESS."
—LAO-TZU

"BUT OH! THE BLESSING IT IS TO HAVE A FRIEND TO WHOM ONE CAN SPEAK FEARLESS ON ANY SUBJECT; WITH WHOM ONE'S DEEPEST AS WELL AS ONE'S MOST FOOLISH THOUGHTS COME OUT SIMPLY AND SAFELY. OH, THE COMFORT—THE INEXPRESSIBLE COMFORT OF FEELING SAFE WITH A PERSON—HAVING NEITHER TO WEIGH THOUGHTS NOR MEASURE WORDS, BUT POURING THEM ALL RIGHT OUT, JUST AS THEY ARE, CHAFF AND GRAIN TOGETHER; CERTAIN THAT A FAITHFUL HAND WILL TAKE AND SIFT THEM, KEEP WHAT IS WORTH KEEPING, AND THEN WITH THE BREATH OF KINDNESS BLOW THE REST AWAY."
—DINAH MARIA MULOCK CRAIK,
A LIFE FOR A LIFE, 1866

CHAPTER 5

EMOTIONAL INTELLIGENCE, SUPPORT, AND LEARNING FROM FAILURE

Learning is both an input and outcome of growing from your failure experiences. As explained in previous chapters, emotions can interfere with your ability to learn from failure. By more effectively managing your emotions, you can minimize this emotional interference to enhance learning. But also, a more effective process of making sense of the failure can enhance your personal growth from the experience. As you will see, those with greater emotional intelligence and those who have access to emotionally intelligent people in their networks are more able to make sense of the failure and grow from the experience.

Making sense of the failure of a project is important to us. We make sense of an event when we go through a process of finding relevant information, interpreting that information, and then assigning meaning to the event to change how we think and act when faced with similar events and situations.[1] This process is ongoing. Previous interpretations of the causes of an event are updated and changed as more information becomes available and is interpreted. This ongoing interpretation often occurs in conjunction with action.[2] Members of a project team experiencing failure go through a process of developing a series of plausible accounts for why the project failed, and each progressive story is more plausible than the previous one.

Scanning is the process by which our attention is allocated to specific features of the internal and external environment. It also involves collecting information arising from this focused attention. Scanning "picks up" information believed to be salient for making sense of a situation. I think of scanning like Tom Hanks searching for rescue craft in the movie *Castaway*. He could scan the horizon from his beach camp or he could climb to the top of the mountain, where he had a 360-degree view of the horizon that surrounded his island. His ability was severely limited while on the beach and substantially expanded while on the mountaintop. The importance of scanning for information is reflected in the old joke about the guy who is searching for his lost keys at night under a street light. When asked why he is looking for his keys under the streetlight and not where he dropped them on his lawn, he responds "Because the light is better over here." His limited scanning is unlikely to yield a positive result.

Scanning refers to where we allocate our attention to capture information about the reasons why the project failed.

Interpretation refers to the process of comprehending the new information that arises as a result of our scanning activities. What do the "bits" of information mean? How do these bits of information fit together? How do they correspond with what we already know? Comprehension is as important to making sense of project failure as it is to reading a book or being on a jury. Comprehension compares new information about the project failure with our existing knowledge about how projects, markets, and technology work.

> Emotion-management strategies *have an impact on the scanning and interpretation of information to change how we act (how and what we learn).*

When the new information does not fit with our prior knowledge, this disconnect provides an opportunity to learn—to revise our prior knowledge by developing a more plausible story that accommodates the new information. By learning new knowledge, we approach the task from a different perspective and/or in a different way. As I will describe (after setting up two illustrative examples), *emotion-management strategies* have an impact on the scanning and interpretation of information to change how we act (how and what we learn). People who are emotionally intelligent are more effective at choosing and implementing these strategies.

Are You Emotionally Intelligent?

More generally, *emotional intelligence* refers to your ability to monitor your own and others' feelings and emotions, to discriminate among them, and to use this information to guide your thinking and actions.[3] How emotionally intelligent are you? Take the survey in Table 5.1. Add up the score for each subscale, and then add up all the scores to get an overall score. To provide some basis for comparison, in a study of 130 fully employed business students at a medium-sized public university, the average score for perception and appraisal of emotions (PA) was 30.1, for facilitating thinking with emotions (FT) was 29.9, for understanding emotions (UE) was 25.5, and for regulating and managing emotions (RE) was 32.4.[4] Figure 5.1 shows the average scores for the student sample, as well as for the people I use as examples in the next section. Plot your score in the last column of Figure 5.1. The bottom box in the column is for perception and appraisal of emotions. Add on top of that a box for FT, and then UE, and finally RE. The total size of the column should correspond to your total score.

If your score on the PA subscale is greater than 30, you have considerable ability to sense and acknowledge your emotions. If your score on the FT subscale is greater than 30, you have considerable control over your emotions. If your score on the UE subscale is greater than 25, you are highly sensitive to the emotions of others and have considerable ability to predict their emotional responses. If your score on the RE subscale is greater than 32, you have considerable ability to direct emotions in positive and productive ways.[5] If your total score is over 118, you have above-average emotional intelligence (at least relative to a group of university students). If it is below this score, the good news is that you can enhance this important ability.

Table 5.1 Measure Your Emotional Intelligence

Using the scale as a guide, circle the number beside each statement to indicate how much you agree with it.

Strongly Disagree					Strongly Agree	
1	2	3	4	5	6	7

Perception and Appraisal of Emotions (PA Subscale)

I can accurately identify a range of emotions that I feel from day to day	1 2 3 4 5 6 7
At work I can instantly tell when someone is frustrating me	1 2 3 4 5 6 7
I can usually imagine what another person is feeling	1 2 3 4 5 6 7
I have no difficulty figuring out how much passion to demonstrate about an issue at work	1 2 3 4 5 6 7
I can usually tell how someone is feeling even though his/her facial expression may conflict with his/her body language	1 2 3 4 5 6 7
I have no difficulty identifying how a person really feels about an issue despite what he/she may say	1 2 3 4 5 6 7

continues

Table 5.1 *(continued)*

Strongly Disagree					Strongly Agree	
1	2	3	4	5	6	7

Facilitating Thinking with Emotions (FT Subscale)

I often prioritize my work tasks according to how strongly I feel about the importance of each task — 1 2 3 4 5 6 7

I often use my excitement about a work project to focus the efforts of others involved with the project — 1 2 3 4 5 6 7

I often use how I feel about a problem to determine how much attention I give it — 1 2 3 4 5 6 7

I listen to the feelings of other people to establish priorities — 1 2 3 4 5 6 7

I deliberately attempt to create a feeling conducive to effective problem solving when meeting with clients or coworkers — 1 2 3 4 5 6 7

In deciding to go forward with a decision, I always consider how other people may feel about it — 1 2 3 4 5 6 7

Understanding Emotions (UE Subscale)

When a coworker performs poorly on a project, I can usually recognize when he/she feels angry, embarrassed, guilty, or some other feeling (such as wounded pride) — 1 2 3 4 5 6 7

I can watch other people interact and recognize the feelings they hold toward each other — 1 2 3 4 5 6 7

I am acutely aware of subtle cues at work that express how people feel (such as where they sit and when they are silent) — 1 2 3 4 5 6 7

I can usually tell when a coworker's emotional response to a situation is due to his/her unique personality instead of his/her cultural background — 1 2 3 4 5 6 7

I can instantly recognize when a coworker's frustrations with a project are escalating — 1 2 3 4 5 6 7

Strongly Disagree					Strongly Agree	
1	2	3	4	5	6	7

Regulating and Management of Emotion (RE Subscale)

I look forward to a feeling of accomplishment whenever I start a new project	1 2 3 4 5 6 7
I am usually able to transmit a sense of enthusiasm about a work project to others	1 2 3 4 5 6 7
I notice when someone is very caring and compassionate toward others at work	1 2 3 4 5 6 7
I am capable to calm someone down who is angry and frustrated at work	1 2 3 4 5 6 7
When a coworker is feeling disappointed about his/her work performance, I make an effort to offer encouraging words of support	1 2 3 4 5 6 7
Whenever painful events have occurred to people I know at work (such as a death in the family or a serious illness), I have expressed genuine concern and tried to help them feel better	1 2 3 4 5 6 7

The scale is from Groves, McEnrue, and Shen.[6]

The higher your score, the more emotionally intelligent you are.

How does this emotional intelligence help you learn and grow from your failure experiences? Specific to project failure, emotional intelligence enables you to effectively use the oscillation model to manage emotions and learn from failure (as detailed in Chapter 2, "Strategies to Learn More from Your Failures"). The more emotionally intelligent you are, the better you are at

- Recognizing the symptoms of your emotions to transition from a loss orientation toward the failed project to a restoration orientation, and vice versa.

- Using your emotions to process information about the failure to learn and grow from the experience.

- Helping other team members recognize the symptoms of their emotions, oscillate between a loss and a restoration orientation, and learn from failure and personally grow from the experience.

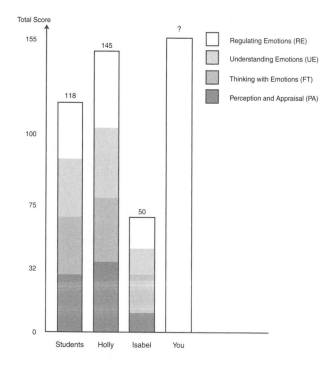

Figure 5.1 Chart your score for emotional intelligence

Growing from the Failure Experience

Two Project Team Leaders with Different Emotional Intelligence

Take two development teams dealing with the failure of their projects (introduced in the previous chapter). The project leader of Pool Be Clean, Holly, and the rest of the team had invested a lot of time, effort, and creativity into this project and felt awful after its termination. Holly was an emotionally intelligent individual. She completed the questionnaire in Table 5.1 and got a high score. (Compare yourself to Holly [PA = 38, FT = 37, UE = 32, RE = 38; total = 145]; see Figure 5.1.)

Isabel was the team leader of Dolphin Away but was not a particularly emotionally intelligent person. She completed the questionnaire in Table 5.1 and scored quite low. (Compare yourself to Isabel [PA = 12, FT = 19, UE = 8, RE = 11; total = 50]; see Figure 5.1.)

Emotions and Scanning for Information

Emotions can provide some positive benefits when we experience a project failure. Emotions signal that something important has been lost. They also signal that the events leading up to that loss are important in explaining why the project failed. These signals

Emotions signal that something important has been lost.

attract attention to information that may be important for understanding why the project failed. These "emotional events" take priority over emotionally neutral events. And events that trigger negative emotions generally receive priority over those that generate positive emotions.

To most of the members of the Pool Be Clean and Dolphin Away teams, the project was very important to them, and they felt bad when it was gone. There was one exception. Brent was a member of the Dolphin Away team who did not care greatly for dolphins, did not care about the fishermen's nets, and really did not buy into the whole "green" movement. This was simply a job. So when the project failed, he did not feel bad; he did not feel joy; he really felt nothing at all. Without his emotions telling him that something important had happened, his focused attention turned to things that were important to him—where he was going for lunch, his shiny sports car parked in the garage, and whether his beloved football team would win the title. His attention turned away from the events leading up to the failure of the Dolphin Away project.

However, it is not just the strength of the emotions we feel that influences our ability to make sense of the project failure, and to grow personally. How we manage these emotions to maximize the scanning for relevant information also matters. The ability to effectively implement these means of managing emotions is influenced by our emotional intelligence.

A *restoration orientation* distracts us from thoughts about the project's failure. Some of this attention may be allocated to scanning for information that helps solve secondary problems—problems that have been created by the project failure. The purpose of this emotion-management strategy is to reduce the emotions generated by the event. To the extent that these "distraction" activities are successful, we and/or the team have diverted attention from the failure event (and events immediately preceding it). Therefore, less (or no) attention is available for scanning for the purposes of making sense of the project failure. For example, the benefit to project leader Holly from searching the classifieds for a new job is that it focuses her attention away from the failure of Pool Be Clean and helps reduce stress related to the possibility of being fired or demoted over the failure. While attention is used to scan the Internet for potential career opportunities, her attention is not allocated to scanning her memory, past test results, and marketing records for information that would be useful in understanding why the project failed.

In contrast to a restoration orientation, a *loss orientation* focuses attention on the failure event and the events leading up to it. This focused attention is important for the purposes of scanning the new information about why the project failed. For example, Isabel was distraught about the failure of Dolphin Away and wanted to know why it had failed. She looked through all the available information—marketing reports, engineering test results, government data on the migration of the bottlenose dolphin and the gray nurse shark. She also searched for new information that might shed light on why the project failed. She interviewed the fishermen who pilot-tested the technology, she spoke with a professor of oceanography at the local university, and she talked to an expert on sonar at the Coast Guard Academy. This scanning for new information could be an important source of information that leads to a more plausible explanation for why the project failed.

However, while a loss orientation enhanced Isabel's scanning for information after an extended period, her attention began to shift from the events leading up to the failure to the emotions at the time of failure and thereafter. She thought about how devastated she was when she heard that the project had been killed and how embarrassed she was at her outburst at top management upon hearing the decision. Her thoughts turned to the dolphins being trapped right now in fishing nets all over the world. This shift in focus toward her thoughts, feelings, and emotions surrounding the project failure means that little attention is free to focus on scanning for new information that will help her make sense of the project failure. This change in focus also increases the strength of our negative emotions and can also decrease cognitive capacity, further reducing scanning activities.

An *oscillation strategy* provides the opportunity to shift from a loss to a restoration orientation when the loss orientation's costs outweigh its benefits for scanning. As Isabel's attention began to focus on her feelings and emotions surrounding the project's failure, she needed to transition to a restoration orientation to take a break from thinking about the project failure so that she could weaken her negative emotions and recharge her cognitive batteries. An oscillation strategy also involves a shift from a restoration orientation to a loss orientation when some secondary problems have been solved and cognitive capacity has returned, ready to be focused, once again, on the events leading up to the failure. After distracting herself by surfing the online job advertisements and finding some interesting possibilities, Holly was less stressed about the possibility of being demoted (or sacked). Her cognitive resources were available to transition to a loss orientation with focused attention on scanning for new information about the reasons for Pool Be Clean's failure.

Emotion and the Interpretation of Information

Information that is noticed as a result of our scanning activities must be interpreted to give it meaning. For example, earlier I mentioned that Isabel searched through government records on the migratory patterns of the bottlenose dolphin and the gray nurse shark but needed to speak with an oceanographer to be able to interpret what these patterns meant for how fishermen used their nets. Therefore, while scanning reveals signals of things that could be important, these signals need to be in a form that allows us to compare them with our existing knowledge and/or the team's existing knowledge.

As discussed, a restoration orientation redirects attention from the events surrounding the failure to unrelated activities—attending a football game—and/or activities designed to solve problems that have arisen as a result of the failure. This can include activities used to try to rebuild legitimacy in the eyes of senior management or to find alternative employment. Both of these help reduce the generation of emotions. Therefore, they can reduce the emotional interference to the information processing necessary to make sense of the failure. However, it requires considerable mental effort to suppress these emotions for an extended period. These thoughts typically rebound and interfere with our ability to make sense of the failure. Furthermore, while these distracter tasks help reduce negative emotions, the interpretation of information that is taking place is with those tasks and not with the task of learning from the failure experience.

A loss orientation allows us to change how we interpret a failure. As a more "plausible story" for the failure is developed, the emotional bonds to the project are broken. A more plausible story is one in which the new and existing information fit together more tightly as a coherent whole. It takes all the bits of information and puts them together in a way that provides the most complete picture. The interpretation of new information into a more plausible account further reduces the emotions generated by thinking about the loss; a reduced emotional reaction frees up information processing capacity. But an extended period of a loss orientation can increase negative emotions. For example, thinking about the failure for an extended time makes negative thoughts more accessible and salient. This can lead to ruminations and make us feel worse. These emotions consume scarce information processing capacity, reducing our ability to interpret new information and make sense of the failure.

❁

I described how Isabel's continued loss orientation led to a focus on her feelings and emotions that surrounded the failure. It also obstructed any further scanning for new information that might be important in shedding light on the reasons for the project's failure. This focus on emotions not only obstructs the scanning for new information, but it also interferes with the processing of information that previously was obtained through scanning. For example, Isabel found a mathematical formula for ocean currents interacting with migration patterns, but she needed a mathematics professor to translate it into words before she could understand what it meant. However, by the time Isabel meets with the mathematics professor, she is in such an emotional state about the deaths of the hundreds of dolphins that have occurred since the project was terminated that she barely hears a word the professor says. She keeps saying, "The dolphins are dying. They're being strangled, and the baby dolphins are being murdered." She walks out of the professor's office with no more useful information than when she walked in.

But an oscillation strategy—transitioning from a loss to a restoration orientation—gives us an opportunity to break the cycle of rumination and restore information processing capacity. Once restored, a transition back to a loss orientation provides an opportunity to again process new information about the loss of the project.

Emotions and Learning

Learning is the final stage of *making sense* of failure. Learning and its subsequent actions are stimulated through scanning and interpretation. The emotion-management strategies, therefore, indirectly affect learning through the impact on scanning and interpretation. In sum, after the project fails, negative emotions run high. These emotions generated from the failure interfere with the scanning, interpretation, and therefore learning from the events surrounding the loss. Therefore:

- Increased **scanning**, **interpretation**, and learning of new information surrounding the failure of the project help you make sense of the loss and enhance personal growth from the failure experience. You can increase your scanning by remaining focused on the task of looking out for signals of new information that could shed light on the causes of the project's failure. You can increase interpretation by more effectively processing that newly scanned information into a form that is comparable with other bits of information you have and with your existing knowledge. You can increase learning by enhancing scanning and interpretation, by changing your activities based on what has made sense so far, and by being open to the possibility of an alternative, more plausible story.

- The use of a **restoration orientation** initially increases scanning, interpretation, and learning, but its extended use eventually decreases the effectiveness of these sense-making mechanisms.

- The use of **loss orientation** initially increases scanning, interpretation, and learning, but its extended use eventually decreases the effectiveness of these sense-making mechanisms.

- The use of **oscillation strategy** increases the scanning, interpretation, and learning of information about the project failure when continued use of one (or the other) orientation starts to detract from your ability to make sense of the failure. Those with greater emotional intelligence are more able to implement an oscillation strategy.

Help from Others and Building Emotional Intelligence

We are rarely alone in the creation and building of a project. A project often needs more than one person to give it life. But when the project fails, many people feel bad. A benefit of a team is that it provides readily identifiable others with whom we can enjoy successes and also share our failures. In sharing our emotions arising from failure, we *may* be able to better manage these emotions and more quickly learn from the experience. There is an opportunity to interact with, and share information with, others who are also feeling bad—an opportunity to help each other deal with, and learn from, the failure experience.

The group dimension of failure is important. First, others can facilitate our emotional management to learn from failure. Second, a project team is more than simply a collection of individuals. The team itself feels loss, can facilitate its learning from failure, and can grow as a team as a result of overcoming this adversity. This assumes that the team remains intact after the project failure to have the opportunity to work as a unit on subsequent projects. Whether or not the project team remains together after the failure, when we experience such an event, we will hopefully remain part of a broader group (social group, family unity, project team, the organization) that provides a source of individuals with whom we can interact and a group structure within which we can learn and grow.

Although we may readily accept the benefit that others provide in helping us deal with emotions, there is still an important skill in being able to make the most of others and one's group. For those who are helping someone manage the emotions generated by failure and learn from the experience, some skills will help them speed this process. It is not an easy task for the receiver or the giver of this emotional help. Some will be better than others.

Social interaction is an important factor in understanding why some who experience project failure can grow while others cannot or are delayed in doing so. For example, a key activity of the loss orientation is to talk through the failure experience. Talking about the events surrounding the loss helps establish a meaning for the failure. The more plausible the account of the failure, the more we can break the emotional bonds to the project. We have all probably been in situations where our accounts of what happened sound great in our heads, but when we say them out loud and open them to the scrutiny of others, we soon realize that our original story was implausible. A social network represents accessible people with whom we can talk through the failure experience. They are an important resource.

However, talking through the experience with others does not always help us make sense of the loss. The "others" can sometimes make things worse. They may say something that increases the negative emotions, which retards personal growth. Knowing this possibility, some people within your social network may become tongue-tied for fear of saying the wrong thing. As a result, the comments come out awkwardly. Alternatively, they say nothing to avoid making things worse.

Therefore, on the one hand, it is important for us to talk to someone. But on the other hand, this is a difficult task for those wanting to help us. It is for this reason that most people turn to their family, friends, and teammates in times of major loss. However, in the case of the failure of a team project, the other team members also often feel bad over the loss. Therefore, some team members are less inclined to support others because they are trying to cope with the loss themselves. How can some people balance their emotional needs with the emotional needs of other team members and grow from the experience, while others are less able and take longer to do so?

The greater our emotional intelligence, the more we can recognize our emotions, recognize others' emotions, and use this information to guide our thinking and actions. That is, we can determine the appropriate emotion-management

> *The greater our emotional intelligence, the more we can recognize our emotions, recognize others' emotions, and use this information to guide our thinking and actions.*

strategy given our current emotional state. We can use the help of others to effectively engage the appropriate orientation and do so without exacerbating the emotions of the "helper." The key is to build our emotional intelligence and make sure that we have emotionally intelligent people in our network.

❊

The important thing to realize is that you are not born with emotional intelligence: you can enhance it. First, enhance your self-awareness of emotions. You can do this by monitoring your emotions. Observe yourself in action, and continuously ask, "How do I feel? How do I feel about the current project? Its performance? The rest of the project team?" Also monitor others' emotions. Observe how they are displaying their emotions and what triggers them. What emotions does a teammate display when he or she is happy, angry, upset, sad?

Second, enhance your ability to manage emotions. Use your enhanced self-awareness of your own and others' emotions to better regulate them. When you realize that you are feeling bad, what activities help stop this feeling from becoming unproductive ruminations? What helps keep them in check? When others are feeling bad, how do they cope? Who is more successful at managing emotions, and why? This is not about eliminating emotions, but enhancing our ability to regulate (manage) them so that the negative consequences are minimized and the benefits are maximized. We can learn to regulate our own emotions, use the help of others to regulate our emotions, and help others manage their emotions.

Mark Magnacca, President of Insight Development Group, runs a motivational program that centers on a *fire walk*—walking across a bed of hot coals—to help participants learn to understand and regulate their emotions and receive the support of others, particularly with their fear of failure. One of his major clients is EMC. I interviewed Mark about a significant event for him and his business:

> "EMC knows that their sales people are going to have some failures before ultimately achieving success. They also realize that it is one thing to talk a big game: 'Don't be fearful of failure' and for people to say 'I can overcome fear.' Fire has this primordial fear about it. The setup is that you do not need to do the fire walk but all I care about is that you support your partner. Between 95 and 99% do the walk. The worst scenario is that you get burned. And if you do, so what? The worst-case scenario is that a few people get a dime-sized blister, and what they realize from that little blister is that I spent a lot of time afraid of this thing and the worst thing that happened is that I got a blister. Let's tough it out and get back on course and make it work."

The lesson that Julie James learned from the fire walk activity is that the only way you get burned is not to try, and that if you can walk on hot coals, you can overcome fear and do it with other aspects of your life.[7] The fire walk represents an example of an activity that promotes the understanding and regulation of emotion and the importance of social support critical to learning from failure. But the fire walk was also the source of a painful failure experience for Mark:

> "EMC has a national sales meeting in Boca Raton, Florida for about two hundred people. When you do a fire walk, it is normally done at night—it is more dramatic. We always use the same kind of wood and the same kind of sod, except for when we went to Florida. What we didn't know was that they did not have oak wood and they did not have Kentucky bluegrass—in Florida they have this Bermuda grass that does not have the dirt underneath it. These are all things that I did not consider because I did not know they mattered. So this time we do the fire walk at high noon. It is so hot this day that it is about 95 and you can see the heat coming off the asphalt. With the fire walk I always go first. I'm leading the group from the front. Behind me is the president of the division and then the national sales manager. I walk and I know from my second step not only that this is hotter than any fire I have ever walked on, but I'm burning. And I

get to the other side and I'm almost in shock at the pain. But I don't know exactly what to do. Before I can even do anything the president walks. Now I can see by the look on his face that he has the same experience as me and now the national sales manager walks— this is the guy that hires me. At this point I can see from both of them that they are suffering what had happened to me. I immediately cut in front of line and say 'Stop, that's it.' I shut it down. I didn't know what had happened, but I knew something bad had happened. Now I have a two-inch blister on the bottom of my foot, a second- or third-degree burn. And so did they. The national sales manager looked at me and said, 'I have to play golf now, but we gotta talk when we get back home.' To his credit he puts his shoes on, in pain, and played 18 holes of golf.

"I go to the airport and walked through the terminal, hobbling on one foot. I have my whole team with me—eight people—they are sort of helping me through the airport. I see EMC people at their respective gates. So it is like the walk of humiliation. We get back home and I see the doctor and he says, 'It is not good but not too bad—but for sure you don't want to walk on any more hot coals.' Basically this business is over.

"I go and see the national sales manager. Expecting for sure he is going to blow me out of the water. He says to me, 'Do you know what happened?' And I say, 'I think I do.' I explained the things I said earlier—the sod, the wood, the ground, the time of the day, it was a confluence of things. He said, 'If you do it again, do you know what to do differently?' I said, 'I think that I do.' Understand at this point I did not want to do it myself. The last thing I wanted to do was walk on hot coals again. What was I going to do—walk with a giant band-aid on? I was hoping that he would just fire me and put me out of my misery. But he didn't. He said, 'I tell you what. We've got the Europeans coming next week, and they have already heard about what had happened. We are going to do it again. And you better get it right. And I'll be there, and I'm going again.' Back I fly down to Florida, still hobbling, but this time we FedEx our own wood, we change the fire walk from high noon to evening, and I get out there as scared as I have ever been, and I walked across this 10-foot bed of hot coals and it did not burn. Nor did I even pop the blister on the bottom of the foot. Then the national sales manager went, and then 250 Europeans. We were back in the game. From that low point of failure, we have had 10,000 people do fire walks."

Mark had learned a lot about his emotions and how to regulate them. He learned from his painful experience and overcame his fear to try again—to do another fire walk while he still had blisters from the previous walk. The national sales manager of EMC also showed great emotional intelligence. I am sure he was angry at Mark, embarrassed by the event, and fearful that he would be burned again. But he was able to regulate these emotions to make an important decision to do the fire walk again. He showed courage by highlighting a tolerance for failure (Mark's failure and perhaps his own for organizing the event in Florida at noon), the importance of learning from the experience, and trying again. Indeed, the national sales manager put his body (feet) on the line, which formed part of an important company story. The underlying message was that if you fail, learn from the experience, and are willing to try again, the management of EMC will stand behind you 100%.

A central theme of the fire walk activity is the support provided by a partner and going through the experience together. Support groups and activities such as the fire walk are means to bring individuals together to interact and help each other manage their emotions. For example, by interacting with others who are also fearful of, and/or feeling bad over, failure, you have the opportunity to learn from them to more effectively perceive, understand, and regulate these emotions.

EMC uses the fire walk as a powerful activity to help employees build their emotional intelligence. The failure in the performance of that activity on one occasion also represents a powerful story that embodies two men's emotional intelligence and a symbol of an organizational culture. This culture promotes team support, overcoming your fears, and learning from failure. By increasing our emotional intelligence, we will be more effective at managing our emotions (including seeking specific social support to help us) to more effectively learn from failure and grow from the experience.

Practical Implications

- Personal growth is greater and is achieved more quickly when you maximize the sense-making dynamics of scanning, interpretation, and learning.

- Sense-making is initially enhanced and then obstructed when using either a loss or restoration orientation for an extended period of time. Oscillating between a loss orientation and a restoration orientation can maximize benefits while minimizing costs in order to maximize learning.

- Team members feel bad over the failure of team projects and use emotion-management strategies to make sense of the failure and grow from the experience. This learning process is enhanced for those who are more emotionally intelligent. They can more effectively use oscillation strategy discussed in Chapter 2 to deal with the emotions of failure.

- Emotional intelligence can be learned and developed so that we can have greater self-awareness and self-regulation of our emotions.

- Use your team and social support to make sense of failure (learn) and to grow from the experience. This should be guided by your emotional intelligence and the emotional intelligence of team members and those in your network.

Conclusion

In this chapter, the failure of a project highlighted the ability to manage the emotions generated by a major loss and the social process of making sense of failure (learning). More emotionally intelligent team members can better recognize and use their emotions and their emotion-management strategies to scan, interpret, and learn from new information about the cause of the project failure. They also are more able to recognize the emotions of other team members and/or others in their network and use them to better manage their own emotions. An organization can offer activities that help its members more effectively engage and disengage their emotions to overcome fear of failure, make sense of failure when it occurs, and build the motivation to try again.

❁

Endnotes

1 Gioia, D.A. and Chittipeddi, K. (1991). "Sense making and sense giving in strategic change initiation." *Strategic Management Journal*, 12: 433–448; Daft, R.L. and Weick, K.E. (1984). "Toward a model of organizations as interpretive systems." *Academy of Management Review*, 9: 284–295; Weick, K. (1979). *The Social Psychology of Organizing*. Reading, MA: Addison-Wesley.

2 Bradley, M.J. (2002). "The right shock to initiate change: A sense making perspective." *Academy of Management Proceedings*, F1–6; Thomas, J.B., Clark, S.M., and Gioia, D.A. (1993). "Strategic sense making and organizational performance: Linkages among scanning, interpretation, action, and outcomes." *Academy of Management Journal*, 36: 239–270.

3 Salovey, P. and Mayer, J.D. (1990). "Emotional intelligence." *Imagination, Cognition and Personality*, 9: 185–211.

4 Groves, K.S., McEnrue, M.P., and Shen, W. (2008). "Developing and measuring the emotional intelligence of leaders." *Journal of Management Development*, 27(2): 225–250.

5 Ibid (Groves); Law, K.S., Wong, C., and Song, L.J. (2004). "The construct and criterion validity of emotional intelligence and its potential utility for management studies." *Journal of Applied Psychology*, 89: 483–496.

6 Groves, K.S., McEnrue, M.P., and Shen, W. (2008).

7 Report by Dave Barker on FOXNews.

"Success is the ability to go from one failure to another with no loss of enthusiasm."
—Sir Winston Churchill
(1874–1965)

"Sometimes life hits you in the head with a brick. Don't lose faith."
—Steve Jobs

"Once you embrace unpleasant news not as negative but as evidence of a need for change, you aren't defeated by it. You're learning from it."
—Bill Gates

CHAPTER 6

PREPARING FOR MULTIPLE FAILURES

The focus so far has been on the emotions triggered by a single project failure to learn and grow from the experience. I have detailed a number of techniques you can use to maximize your learning from this specific failure event. If you're motivated to try again, you can apply what you have learned to enhance the likelihood that your next project will succeed. In this chapter, I acknowledge that in some work contexts, project failure is a common occurrence. Not only do you need tools for coping with one project failure, but you also need an approach for managing emotions across multiple project failures. How do you maintain your commitment to project success when you know that project failure (and its accompanying emotions) is likely?

The more committed you are to a project, the less likely it will fail, but the worse you will feel if it does fail. The less committed you are to a project, the less bad you will feel if it fails, but the greater the likelihood that it will fail. Why can some people make the considerable commitment necessary for project success while quickly learning from their experiences if the project fails, but others are unable or slow to do so?

Commitment and Performance

Although projects can take many varied forms, project success depends on commitment—the commitment of management, the project leader, and the rest of the project team. The project begins with a creative idea. Our creativity is greater for ideas about which we are passionate.[1] For example, Eddie works for a sports equipment manufacturer called SEM. In particular, he is passionate about skateboarding, Rollerblading, and cross-country skiing. His deep interest in and knowledge of these hobbies provided him the creative resources needed to invent the Skiing Scooter. The Skiing Scooter is a three-wheeled device (one in the front and two in the back) with a flexible frame. The rider pushes out with one leg and then the other leg in a motion similar to cross-country skiing. The Skiing Scooter is propelled solely by the efforts of the rider. It has been clocked at a maximum speed of 45 miles an hour on a flat road.

Even the best-conceived projects face obstacles that require persistence to overcome and move closer to success. A primary determinant of persistence is our commitment to the project. Without commitment, a project has little chance of achieving success. Eddie was committed to the success of the Skiing Scooter. Although top management of SEM were skeptical about the Skiing Scooter, Eddie convinced them to invest $150,000 to develop prototypes and

> *Without commitment, a project has little chance of achieving success.*

test the product's viability. Excited about the prototypes, Eddie took the Skiing Scooter to skateboard shops to see if they would be interested in selling it in their stores. The first store he went to said no. The second store also said no. After he had visited 50 skateboard stores, the answer was still no. But Eddie wouldn't take no for an answer. He believed in this product; he just had to find a way to make it work. He visited bike stores and received the same answer from them—no. But then he found that a large chain of ski stores was very interested in selling this product because their customers were cross-country skiers who bought things only during the winter. This was a chance to offer them a product for the rest of the year.

Despite considerable commitment by team members, projects can still fail. For example, perhaps the market did not grow as expected, the anticipated technological benefits did not materialize, and/or the project was preempted by a competitor. In Eddie's case, the outward pressure applied by the rider to propel the Skiing Scooter was so great that it was causing deformation and cracking in the frame. Despite many attempts to strengthen the frame, this engineering challenge was too great. Eddie was forced to kill the Skiing Scooter project. Regardless of how or why the project failed, those committed to the project will feel they have lost something important. For example, they have lost the emotional bond to the future product or the markets the projects represented, they have lost some of their self and collective identity, and/or they have lost key working relationships with others on the now-disbanded team. Eddie had lost his dream of walking down the street and being passed by kids flying by on their Skiing Scooters. Eddie felt bad about the failure of this project. So did the others who had worked with him on the project.

The project team members feel an attachment to the projects to which they are committed. When that attachment is broken, they experience negative emotions. This is illustrated well by the following quote from Albert Yu, senior vice president of Intel. He acknowledges the emotions generated by failure and highlights the opportunities to learn from experience:

> "… the infamous Pentium flaw in 1994 was devastating, and we went through all the stages of grief—denial, anger, acceptance. It

was incredibly painful to the company and to me, personally. But we managed to become better as a result. It marked a real transition. I'm a different person today. I've beefed up the way we validated technology before it gets out the door. We went from having a product-engineered orientation to a consumer orientation. We broke down barriers inside the company because we were all involved in an emergency."[2]

❋

As I have detailed in previous chapters, emotions interfere with learning from failure experiences. They interfere with scanning for new information to help to make sense of the failure. They also interfere with your ability to interpret information about the cause of the project's failure. This emotional interference is potentially debilitating for learning from failure given the often highly complex reasons behind the event and the motivation necessary to overcome obstacles.

Holly Hogan was brought to Energizer to launch a tester that indicated how much power remained in a battery.[3] This on-battery tester would be a really big deal in the battery world. However, Energizer experienced numerous R&D hiccups. Days before meeting with the executive board to obtain final approval for the launch, Holly recalls R&D coming to her office and saying that there was a problem with the tester:

"The problem was that if the battery was over 10% good, it would still register as good but could die within five minutes of putting the battery in. And I flipped out. So we are Energizer and we stand for long-lasting and we keep going and going; we can't have a tester that doesn't register properly and gives people bad information. R&D, being scientists, say technically the test is accurate—it's still good, just not for an extended period. I was devastated, absolutely devastated, because that was what I was hired to do, and here it was five years later and we had to make the recommendation to the executive board that we should not go forward."

As Holly recalls, the president of Energizer sat down with her after the meeting and said, "First of all, this is not your problem. We know what happened here with the technology. The reason that you are in this position is because you are so passionate. And the reason this will succeed, if we can ever get it fixed, is because of your passion. So while you feel miserable, and I can see it in your face, I ask that you not let anyone else know how you are feeling. You are the cheerleader, you are the brand person, and I want you to come in tomorrow and act as if nothing has happened." Holly found this to be a "fabulous pep talk."

After restructuring the team and overcoming problems in communication between marketing and R&D, they were able to fix the problem and launch the product. Holly learned that "The personal-emotional can get in the way of success. He [the president] saw that, and he was willing to step in and help me through that. The R&D team was not necessarily devastated. They did not get why I was so upset. They did not get the consumer implication of it." The president of Energizer wanted to take any negative emotions out of the process and keep the positive—keep the passion. But as I will discuss later in this chapter, eliminating emotion as an output (negative emotional reaction) while keeping it as an input (passionate commitment to a project) is a difficult task to achieve.

Managing Failure by Normalizing It

Learning from Small Wins

When the consequences of failure are high, complex tasks can be broken into a series of more modest ones.[4] This gives you the opportunity to experience a number of *small wins*. These small wins help you build a self-belief (and a belief within the team) that you can be successful with this task and enhance performance on more difficult project tasks. We do this with children all the time to teach them to read, play baseball, and swim. For reading, we start them off with short books that have large pictures and few words. For baseball we start with a small bat and a tee to hold the ball in place. For swimming, we start by teaching them to blow bubbles and put their face in the water. We do not start them on *War and Peace*, pitch them curveballs, or play water polo. By getting a chance to have some small wins by finishing a book, hitting the ball, and putting their head under the water, they can feel that they have accomplished something, that they were successful, and that they will be successful at the next stage—the next level of difficulty. This confidence in their ability to succeed means that they will persist longer at the task and are more likely to achieve success. In contrast, the "throw them in the deep end" method of teaching a child to swim exposes the child to the "full" swimming experience but likely shakes their confidence such that they dislike swimming and won't walk within fifty yards of a pool.

However, a limitation of the small wins approach is that it may be difficult to break down complex tasks. For example, you can break down skydiving all you like, but to perform the task, you need to jump out of a plane. Similarly, it was difficult for Eddie to start with smaller steps. The only way he could figure out whether people would buy the Skiing Scooter and determine that it could be made was to make some. There was no viable intermediate step. Furthermore, the smallness of the wins may not capture much of our attention. Although learning to blow bubbles may capture the attention of a two-year-old, it is unlikely to entertain Olympic gold medalists Ian Thorpe and Michael Phelps. Eddie wasn't that interested in conducting basic research on the latent demands of skateboarders before moving ahead with his project. (Besides, it turned out that this is not where the market was anyway—it was cross-country skiers in the summer.) With little attention focused on the tasks, there is less scanning for new information and less processing of that information (see Chapter 5, "Emotional Intelligence, Support, and Learning from Failure").

Learning from Intelligent Failure

An alternative to the small wins approach is *intelligent failure*. This approach acknowledges the learning benefits that arise from experiencing failure. The project team members can learn from failure when the following occurs. First, the project needs to be the result of thoughtfully planned actions. The thoughtful plan provides the basis for comparison with the events that led to the failed outcome. It represents the benchmark from which learning will occur. Second, the project must have had an uncertain outcome. There must have been a chance for the project to be successful (at least when it was created). Learning provides an explanation for why the outcome deviated from expectations and thus reduces the uncertainty for similar projects in the future. Third, the projects are of modest size. It is good to learn from failure, but keep the tuition low. But it needs to be of sufficient size to capture your attention. Fourth, the project and its failure need to be approached from a nonemotional perspective. The failure of projects should not produce a negative emotional reaction. Finally, the project needs to be in a field that corresponds with your current knowledge base.[5] That knowledge base provides the basis for absorbing new information generated by the failure.

The key to the intelligent failure approach is that it requires you to approach project failure from a nonemotional state. Jim Parker, former CEO of Southwest Airlines, was able to approach failures from a nonemotional state and created a culture where others did also:

> *"I am a lawyer by trade. If you try cases, you lose some and you win some. I can't say I learned more from losing a case other than you are going to go on and win your share of cases. It was a great experience for business. It teaches you the importance of leveling out your emotions and not getting too high or too low. ... As a leader you encourage others to do the best they can, and if it doesn't work, you just learn from it and go on. It gives people the opportunity to go out and make decisions and take risks. Make mistakes, and learn to accept that. It makes for a more vibrant organization."*

You can learn to become emotionless (the extreme version of "leveling out your emotions," and therefore not necessarily what Parker advocates) when you normalize failure. You normalize failure when you render the extraordinary (in this case, failure) ordinary. That is, you create the context in which you see the project's failure as a normal, ordinary event. The process of normalization means that a stimulus that would have been perceived as threatening, consequential, and/or personally meaningful is now perceived as less threatening, less salient, and less arousing. Google cofounder Larry Page is an example of a leader who encourages people not to feel bad about failure and perhaps even feel good about it. For example, Sheryl Sandberg, a vice president at Google, made a mistake that cost the company millions of dollars. She felt terrible about it. In response to being told about the mistake, Page expressed pleasure. He was pleased because he realized that mistakes reflect a company that is moving quickly, trying to do too much, and taking plenty of risks. This is the type of company he wanted.[6]

Normalizing failure so that you can become emotionless to project failure can be implemented through repeated exposure to failure. Repeated exposure to failure progressively weakens the negative emotional reaction to it.

> *Repeated exposure to failure progressively weakens the negative emotional reaction to it.*

A special form of repeated exposure is the process of *desensitization*. To desensitize yourself to failure, expose yourself to failures of increasing magnitude. The mismatch between the expected failure and the actual failure is small. Therefore, each new failure generates a lesser emotional reaction than would otherwise have been the case without this process of desensitization. These processes lead to normalizing failure. Normalizing failure can enhance persistence and performance on highly undesirable tasks.

For example, Kathy worked as a new-product development team leader for ToyCo. She would develop and then test the market viability of new games for children. Historically, only 10% of the games that are developed and tested make it to store shelves. Even fewer are big hits. When Kathy started at ToyCo, she poured her heart and soul into the development of a new board game for teenagers. After she had invested three weeks of her time and $25,000, top management terminated the project. Kathy was upset, but she moved on to another project, which also failed. Since that time she has experienced hundreds of project failures. They are commonplace. Now she manages projects that last six months or more and cost hundreds of thousands of dollars. When they fail, she hardly feels a thing. It is part of doing business in a dynamic, highly competitive industry. She no longer becomes downhearted by a failure. Indeed, after the death of one project, she can immediately turn all her attention to the next one.

To most of us, project failure is an undesirable outcome at work. By normalizing failure, you can enhance persistence with innovation efforts into subsequent projects. It also removes the emotional interference to learning from the failure experience. One of Kathy's friends, Curley, was unable to detach his emotions from the failures, and top management decided that this line of business was too tough for such a sensitive person. His emotions were interfering with his work at ToyCo.

Challenges of Normalizing Failure

There are two primary challenges to the effective use of normalizing the failure of projects, such as that employed by ToyCo.

First, the outcomes of normalizing failure that provide its reported benefits may also be its greatest obstacle. By eliminating the emotions triggered by failure, Kathy eliminated the emotional interference to learning from experience. However, in doing so, she also eliminated the benefits of learning that arise from such emotional reactions. That is, if you change failure from a negative emotional event to an emotionally neutral event, the failure event loses its emotional significance. Emotional significance means that something important has been lost, which triggers an urgency to understand why the event occurred.

If failure does not trigger an emotional reaction, this induces only a low level of attention to the event. There will be less scanning for new information about why the failure occurred. Less interpretation of new information will occur, because attention is allocated to other tasks and activities. As a result, less learning takes place. Feelings and emotions let us know that something important has happened, that we must allocate attention to make sense of the loss. Therefore, we need to recognize both the benefits and costs of emotions of learning from failure.

For example, although Curley may have become disheartened with a project failure, this emotional reaction captured and focused his attention on understanding why the project failed. Doing so enabled him to scan for new information about the project's performance and process that information to gain a deeper understanding of the why the project failed. This deeper understanding of this one project failure may offer some keys that could be used to avoid similar problems with similar projects in the future. In contrast, Kathy was able to quickly detach herself from the failed project and throw herself into the next project. With little emotion attached to the project lost, she allocated all her attention to the new project and none to reflecting on why the previous project failed. She had little chance of learning anything from the failure and therefore was likely to make the same mistakes again.

Second, normalization reduces, and eventually eliminates, emotion as an output of the organizational process. Eliminating it as an output can limit the investment of emotional resources as an input into the process. That is, by reducing the emotional importance of the loss of the project, you also lose some of the emotional importance of creating and sustaining your projects. This reduced emotional commitment to projects after normalizing failure reduces the commitment necessary for innovations and motivations for their success. Less creativity and less commitment from the project leader and team members are all associated with poor project performance.[7]

The following quote from Pearl Buck highlights the relationship between emotion as an input and as an output of the creative process:

> "The truly creative mind in any field is no more than this: a human creature born abnormally, inhumanly sensitive. To him, a touch is a blow, a sound is a noise, a misfortune is a tragedy, a joy is an ecstasy, a friend is a lover, a lover is a god, and failure is death. Add to this cruelly delicate organism the overpowering necessity to create, create, create—so that without the creating of music or poetry or books or buildings or something of meaning, his very breath is cut off from him. He must create, must pour out creation. By some strange, unknown, inward urgency he is not really alive unless he is creating."

Desensitizing such a person to the emotions of failure outcomes might eliminate the individual's emotional investment and "strangle" his or her creativity. This is what appeared to happen to Kathy.

She is now hardened to the failure of projects. The byproduct of this is that she makes less of an emotional investment in the creation and management of new projects. With less emotional investment, these projects have a greater likelihood of failure.

We can think of normalizing failure as analogous to a doctor treating cancer patients. The doctor can become desensitized to death. This could be purely the result of the numbers of deaths (of patients or projects) he faces each year. But it likely represents a mechanism to protect himself from feeling bad. This protective mechanism is consistent with normalizing failure. However, to the extent that the doctor desensitizes himself to the death of patients, he engages in depersonalization. Depersonalization is a means of desensitizing oneself to death. Doctors who depersonalize their patients have poorer communication with their patients and the patients' families. In one study, doctors who depersonalized their patients had communications with patients and patients' families that were negative, callous, and otherwise excessively detached.[8] Such behaviors associated with doctors who depersonalize their patients lead to less effective patient care.

Regulating Emotion to Cope with Failure

An alternative to normalizing failure to eliminate emotions is to regulate these emotions. Emotion regulation is the process of coping with high levels of negative emotion triggered by failure by managing them. The next section explores how we can better cope with these emotions—how to mobilize motivation, cognitive resources, and actions to personally grow from failure. We can personally grow in a way that enables us to learn from the experience and be motivated to reinvest emotional resources in subsequent projects.

Your Ability to Cope

People differ in how they function when faced with a trauma. Some cope well, and others do not. Coping involves thoughts and actions that you use to manage the demands of a stressful situation. These demands are external, such as pressure from creditors, customers, and other stakeholders. These demands are also internal, such as anxiety, distress, and ruminations. The coping process is triggered when you believe that something important is threatened or lost. Here, we are focused on coping with the loss of a project when it is terminated for poor performance.

We assess activities in terms of whether they are within, or exceed, our coping capabilities. If you believe you can succeed at a work-related task, you are more likely to engage in that task and succeed at it. The same goes for coping with project failure. If you believe you can successfully cope with the loss of something important or with a threatening situation, you are more likely to have a go at this challenging task even if loss is possible. Our interests are in failure and the regulation of emotions. Therefore, we focus on *coping ability* as the skill to manage the negative emotions generated from failure. Curley, formerly from ToyCo, had low coping abilities. He perceived a large gap between his ability to cope with the emotions generated by failure and what was required to successfully move on. Because he believed he was unable to cope with project failure, the nature of the threat of another project failure was magnified in his mind. This increased his level of worry and stress. That is, he acknowledged the threat associated with the uncertainty of project outcomes—the likelihood of failure—and began to magnify the anticipated emotional hurt from the failure. Those with low coping ability focus their thoughts on the possible negative outcomes of failure and feel powerless to relieve their minds of these thoughts.[9]

Eddie from SEM had a strong belief in his ability to cope with failure and to grow from it. He did not carry the same cognitive burden of thoughts focused on the negative emotional outcomes of uncertain projects as did Curley. He also felt he had greater control over these emotions, could rid his mind of destructive thoughts, and was proactive about engaging in activities that make the task of exploring new projects less threatening.

In one study of trauma survivors after Hurricane Opal, Benight and colleagues found that the level of the survivors' self-reported coping ability was a key factor in determining whether the trauma led to enduring distress.[10] Those with high coping ability more quickly recovered from the trauma, and those with low coping ability were more likely to experience longer-term psychological problems. Consistent with this study, Eddie was more likely to perceive threats as less threatening, exhibit lower levels of stress, engage in less rumination, enact better strategies for dealing with threats, and learn more quickly from them than was Curley.[11]

Differences in people's coping ability helps explain why some are better able to learn from failure and personally grow from the experience. Those with high coping ability are better able to regulate emotions to learn from failure. Coping ability plays a key role in explaining the stress in anticipation of the potential failure and the effectiveness of coping strategies for dealing with emotions after failure occurs. The negative aspects of emotions on learning are diminished for those with high coping ability and are magnified for those with low coping ability. Curley was not in a good position to learn from his failure experiences, because the additional anxiety and stress created by his realization about his low coping ability further interfered with the learning process.

Therefore, for those with high coping ability, learning from failure increases with emotions, because they benefit from the pros of an emotional reaction to failure while minimizing its costs. However, there is a level of emotions at which further increases overwhelm the person's coping ability, and learning outcomes diminish.

Knowing that you can cope with the downside of a project can be quite liberating.

Facing emotions from failure, and successfully managing them, not only facilitates learning from the experience but also gives you the confidence to commit your emotional resources to subsequent projects. Knowing that you can cope with the downside of a project can be quite liberating, because it allows you to make the sort of emotional commitment necessary for subsequent success. Eddie could make a full emotional commitment to the Skiing Scooter despite knowing that there was a high likelihood of failure. He believed that even though he knew he would feel bad if it failed, he had the skills to be able to manage these emotions and learn from the experience. However, Curley was less willing to invest his emotional resources and less committed to subsequent projects. As a result, failure became more likely. It is not surprising that Curley left ToyCo.

❂

The following is an example of how experiencing multiple failures does not necessarily mean that failure generates a weaker emotional response but that the emotional pain and suffering do not last as long: When he was interviewed by *BusinessWeek* and asked, "Does it ever become easier to fail?"

Nicholas Hall, entrepreneur and former president of the Silicon Valley Association of Startup Entrepreneurs, responded, "What does become easier is to bounce back. That's really the most important thing—to get back up at the plate and to start to understand over time it's just part of the process."[12]

Coping ability only explains differences in learning and commitment outcomes for those who regulate emotions. For those who normalize failure, project failure does not generate a negative emotional reaction and therefore is not a threat that needs to be "coped with" in advance. We do not know whether Kathy has high or low coping abilities. It does not matter. Given that project failure does not generate emotions, she does not need to draw on (or think about drawing on) her coping skills. There is nothing to cope with, because failure is not seen as emotionally threatening.

From the preceding statement, a simple prescription is that for those with low coping abilities, like Curley, learning from failure and commitment to subsequent projects will be enhanced by normalizing failure. Only those who have high coping ability, like Eddie, should regulate emotions to maximize learning and maintain commitment. However, such a "simple" prescription assumes that coping ability is an enduring personality trait that cannot be developed. Such an assumption is incorrect. Curley could have developed his coping abilities and become more like Eddie.

The next section explores how you can enhance your coping ability and emotion regulation. Psychologists have long recognized the benefits of groups to the process of making sense of loss (see Chapter 5)—in particular, the social support offered by support groups and in following rituals, such as funerals. You and your team can use both of these to regulate emotions generated by project failure.[13]

Use Support Groups and Other Social Support

The *self-help group* is a common form of social support. Self-help groups are led by a peer who has previously faced a major loss and successfully managed the emotions from it. The leader is not a professional (psychologist), and his or her role is not to act as counselor or therapist. Rather, the role of the leader is to facilitate discussion between members of the support group. This group discussion gives you the opportunity to share information about your thoughts, feelings, and coping strategies—what seems to work and what does not—and to receive (and give) emotional support from (to) others in the group. Self-help support groups represent a low-cost, low-threat environment to receive social support, learn coping skills, and gain the confidence you need to face new challenges.[14]

Earlier in the chapter, we discussed doctors' depersonalization and normalizing death and the negative consequences this has on patient care. In a study of 816 oncology care providers, those who received social support from colleagues were more able to cope with the emotional demands of the job without becoming callous, indifferent, or otherwise detached from their patients.[15]

Although it is easy to imagine self-help support groups in hospices, where death is a common occurrence, they are not uncommon in firms. Indeed, support groups exist in firms to help employees deal with specific threats that exist outside the workplace and that negatively impact performance at work. For example, support groups are offered in firms for alcohol abuse, marital problems, and the death of loved ones.[16] Some firms offer support groups to help individuals cope with threats generated by the firm. For example, firms have created support groups to help members cope with perceived threats of massive change efforts.[17]

Self-help groups can play a role in developing the coping ability of their members by offering them support. The good news is that Curley joined SEM. SEM's rate of failure for new projects is about the same as the one for ToyCo, but Curley attends a support group run by Eddie. This support group acts as an enabler of learning and action. It provides Curley, and the other members, a basis from which to model his coping attitudes and skills. He could see that, with perseverance, the emotional challenges associated with failures are surmountable. He also felt motivated by the opportunities for personal growth, including learning from the experience. This social support has helped build Curley's coping ability. It also has helped him more effectively learn from failure and remain committed to subsequent projects.

Individuals who feel bad over project failure can seek existing support groups within their organization or create one for this purpose. Eddie created the first self-help group at SEM, and now there are five of them. These groups may not be formal or even fully formed. For example, "Realizing that his food-processing company was swiftly approaching its demise, James Kilmer set up a lunch with several local entrepreneurs who had failed, 'so I knew what to expect,' he says. 'One had had some problems dealing with banks and secured lenders. Another guy had bounced back. It gave me hope.'"[18]

Use Rituals

Rituals represent "standardized, detailed sets of techniques and behaviors that the culture prescribes to manage anxieties and express common identities."[19] A funeral ritual is a specific type of ritual over the loss of a loved one that can provide some benefits to the survivors. They are symbolic events that help the survivor make sense of the failure and witness the grieving of others who share similar feelings about the lost loved one. A funeral also highlights the impact on the community and that the community will continue in his or her absence.[20]

The benefits of funeral rituals may extend beyond the loss of a loved one in a community to the loss of something important within an organization, such as parting ceremonies for displaced workers caused by organizational death. The following quote from Harris and Sutton makes the case for having a parting ceremony—such as a formal social event that arises in response to the imminent breaking of social bonds—in response to or, ideally, in anticipation of a business's death:

> *The death of an organization causes the loss of an important network of mutual obligations. It destroys a major social arena in which members have spent much of their time. Because of this loss, a closing is emotionally charged; it causes mourning, anger, depression, sorrow, and fear of the unknown, the future, and the ambiguous present. The events leading to the death of an organization and the demise itself place strong demands on members to make sense of an unfamiliar stream of events.*[21]

Parting ceremonies provide emotional support for the workers and facilitate an adjustment to their thinking. These purposes are achieved through eleven common elements that occur across the parties analyzed. Participants do the following:

- Exchange phone numbers and e-mail addresses.
- Promise to keep in touch.
- Consume food and alcoholic beverages.
- Express sadness.

- Express anger.
- Invite former members to attend.
- Discuss their own future with others.
- Tell each other that it is really over.
- Discuss the causes of the organization's demise.
- Tell stories about the "old place."
- Take photographs.[22]

Consider this invitation to a "wake" for a dying organization as an example of how emotions can be regulated to positive effect:

> *The wake is to be an occasion to remember the vigor and charm of the departing spirit. We are interested in recalling and sharing memories of the place with those who were its friends and who may have benefited from their association with it over the years. If you cannot attend, please consider sending a message, perhaps containing an anecdote you remember with pleasure.*[23]

In short, as projects die, (former) project team members are likely to do two things. They have a negative emotional response to that loss, and they mourn. They also benefit from the emotional support provided by the rituals of parting ceremonies because these ceremonies help them cope with the loss. For example, Ore-Ida, a subsidiary of H.J. Heinz, shot off a cannon in celebration when it identified a "perfect failure." Another company "established a 'Golden Turkey Award' that was given quarterly, with a lighthearted yet serious spirit, to the individual or team with the greatest 'innovation failure.'"[24] The Marines also celebrate their successes and failures. For example, every month one commander gives out the "toilet seat award" for the individual who displayed the most initiative with a project that had an unsuccessful outcome. The recipients value the award. It tells the group that it is important to be creative, take a chance, and act.[25]

It could be that such rituals represent a "simple recognition that all research and development is inherently risky, that the only way to succeed at all is through lots of tries, that management's primary objective should be to induce lots of tries, and that a good try that results in some learning is to be celebrated even when it fails."[26] Such an explanation is consistent with intelligent failure. However, the perspective of learning from failure at Intuit offers a different explanation for the effectiveness of such a ritual.

✦

Intuit created a marketing campaign that failed. It believed that a hip-hop theme and a website called RockYourRefund.com would attract young clients to its tax filing business. But Intuit was wrong. The team that created the failed concept was presented an award for their efforts by the firm's chairman. Chairman Scott Cook emphasized that it is a bad outcome only if the company fails to learn from the experience. At Intuit, each failed project goes through a postmortem to help people understand why a project failed. Intuit also runs sessions called "When Learning Hurts" and provides information about failures so that employees can "feel the pain" of failure.[27]

At Intuit these rituals after a project failure provide a meeting place where social exchange can offer the members support after they have experienced the failure. They also can hear about how others experience failure and cope effectively with it. At these "When Learning Hurts" sessions, individuals can express their emotions of sadness, anger, disappointment, and so on that were triggered when the project failed. They also can reminisce about the project that used to be (by sharing stories and photographs) and discuss the causes of its demise. As others join in, this helps them overcome denial (for example, they can admit that "it's really over"). It also directs their attention such that scanning is focused on information that is important in learning from the failure experience. These rituals are a chance for team members of failed projects to share stories of past failures and how they were able to cope with the loss and move on. Rituals involving loss stimulate the social sharing of emotions, helping to improve the coping abilities of those present. Therefore, the shooting of a cannon, a failure award, a failure party, or any other ritual that symbolizes the death of a project is most effective in enhancing learning from failure when it provides a means for building your coping ability.

Although parting or funeral rituals are likely to provide a net positive effect, there are some possible negative consequences. By encouraging people to express their emotions of sadness and anger, reminisce about the project that used to be, discuss the causes of the demise, and focus on the symptoms of distress, the circumstances surrounding these symptoms may come to dominate individuals' thoughts and emotions. This makes the experienced threat more salient and future commitment to subsequent projects less likely.[28] It may be beneficial to use rituals to also encourage oscillation to a restoration (versus loss) orientation, where individuals avoid further thoughts about the failure and are proactive toward other aspects of their lives and work. For example, institute a "spring cleaning" ritual. The team comes together to collect and store all the belongings of the deceased project as a way of dealing with a difficult task, reducing a secondary stressor, and symbolizing readiness to move on.

Comparing "Normalizing" and "Regulating" Failure

Emotions, positive and negative, impact your ability to learn from the failure experience and remain committed to subsequent projects. If you normalize failure, you can reduce or even eliminate the emotions triggered by failure. This eliminates the emotional interference on the learning process. However, there are some costs. It also eliminates the attention that emotional events receive, which inhibits aspects of learning. In addition, by eliminating emotion as an output of projects, it can also reduce your emotion as an input (commitment) to subsequent projects, increasing the likelihood of their failure.

Individuals who regulate emotions build their coping ability through social support groups and rituals so that they can maximize the benefits and minimize the costs of emotions on learning from failure experiences. With an ability to cope with the negative emotions generated by project failure, the threat of failure is not as great, and you are more willing to invest your emotional resources in subsequent projects. The success of the regulation approach depends on building your coping ability.

Practical Implications

- The effectiveness of an approach to failure depends on the extent of your ability to cope with, and manage, an emotional reaction to failure (high coping ability).

- For those with low coping ability, the normalizing approach to failure may be the most effective. This approach does not rely on your coping ability. Regulation is more effective for those with high coping ability and those who can develop their coping ability.

- You can enhance the effectiveness of the regulation approach by developing and using routines that provide social support and rituals for building coping ability.

- You can enhance the effectiveness of the normalizing failure approach through communications, policies, and norms that reinforce how common failure is, how it is to be expected, and that it is no big deal.

- Learning from failure is important, but you must be willing to (re)invest in subsequent projects for this new knowledge to be important.

- How you manage the emotions that are the outcome of failure will influence your emotional investments in subsequent projects. The lower your emotional investment in (commitment to) subsequent projects, the more likely the project will fail.

Conclusion

Failures provide us an opportunity to learn. We see that there are numerous challenges in managing emotions that generate failure. You considered two approaches to managing this challenge. The first is normalizing failure to eliminate emotions, and the second acknowledges emotions and regulates them. Both approaches offer different benefits to and costs of learning from failure and personally growing from the experience. Regulation depends on building our coping ability. You explored how support groups and rituals provide the social support necessary to build this important emotional resource.

Endnotes

[1] Amabile, T.M. (2000). "Stimulate creativity by fueling passion." *Blackwell Handbook of Principles of Organizational Behavior*, 331–341. Malden, MA: Blackwell Business.

[2] Dillon, P. (1998). "Failure is just part of the culture of innovation: Accept it and become stronger." www.fastcompany.com/online/20/yu.html.

[3] Name changed to maintain anonymity.

[4] Weick, K.E. (1984). "Small wins: Redefining the scale of social problems." *American Psychologist*, 39: 40–49.

[5] Sitkin, S.B. (1992). "Learning through failure: The strategy of small losses." *Research in Organizational Behavior*, 14: 231–266; 243.

[6] Lashinsky, A. (2006). "Chaos by design: The inside story of disorder, disarray, and uncertainty at Google. And why it's all part of the plan. (They hope.)." *Fortune*, October 2, 2006.

[7] Amabile, T.M. (2000). "Stimulate creativity by fueling passion." *Blackwell Handbook of Principles of Organizational Behavior*, pp. 331–341; Song, X.M. and Parry, M.E. (1997). "A cross-national comparative study of new product development processes: Japan and the United States." *Journal of Marketing*, 61: 1–18.

[8] Peeters, M.C.W. and Le Blanc, P.M. (2001). "Towards a match between job demands and sources of social support: A study among oncology care providers." *European Journal of Work & Organizational Psychology*, 10(1): 53–72.

9 Bandura, A. (1997). *Self-Efficacy: The Exercise of Control*. New York: W.H. Freeman and Company; Lazarus, R.S. and Folkman, S. (1984). *Stress, Appraisal, and Coping*. New York: Springer.

10 Benight, C.C., Swift, E., Sanger, J., Smith, A., and Zeppelin, D. (1999). "Coping ability as a prime mediator of distress following a natural disaster." *Journal of Applied Social Psychology*, 29: 2443–2464.

11 Benight, C.C. and Bandura, A. (2003). "Social cognitive theory of traumatic recovery: The role of perceived self-efficacy." *Behaviour Research and Therapy*, 42: 1129–1148.

12 Kurtz (2005). "Failure is part of success." Businessweek.com, June 22, 2005.

13 Shepherd, D.A., Covin, J., and Kuratko, D. "Project failure from corporate entrepreneurship: Managing the grief process." *Journal of Business Venturing* (forthcoming).

14 Caserta, M.S. and Lund, D.A. (1993). "Intrapersonal resources and the effectiveness of self-help groups for bereaved older adults." *The Gerentologist*, 33: 619–629.

15 Peeters, M.C.W. and Le Blanc, P.M. (2001). "Towards a match between job demands and sources of social support: A study among oncology care providers." *European Journal of Work & Organizational Psychology*, 10(1): 53–72.

16 Kahnweiler, W.M. and Riordan, R.J. (1998). "Job and employee support groups: Past and prologue." *The Career Development Quarterly*, 47: 173–187.

17 Esty, H. (1987). "The management of change." *Employee Assistance Quarterly*, 2: 89–97.

18 Useem, J. (1998). "Failure: The secret of my success." www.inc.com/magazine/19980501/922.html.

19 Trice, H.M. and Beyer, J.M. (1993). *The Cultures of Work Organizations*. Englewood Cliffs, NJ: Prentice-Hall.

20 Fulton, R. (1988). "The funeral in contemporary society." In H. Wass, F.M. Berardo, and R.A. Neimeyer (eds.), *Dying: Facing the Facts* (pp. 257–277). New York: Hemisphere.

21 Harris, S.G. and Sutton, R.I. (1986). "Functions of parting ceremonies in dying organizations." *Academy of Management Journal*, 29: 5–30 (page 11).

22 Harris, S.G. and Sutton, R.I. (1986). "Functions of parting ceremonies in dying organizations." *Academy of Management Journal*, 29: 5–30.

23 Ibid.

24 Kaplan, S. (2008). "Creating a culture for innovation: Driving innovation through strategic changes to organizational culture." www.1000advices.com/guru/innovation_culture_sk.html.

25 Santamaria, J.A., Martino, V., and Clemons, E.K. (2005). *The Marine Corps Way: Using Maneuver Warfare to Lead a Winning Organization*. New York: McGraw-Hill.

26 Peters, T.J. and Waterman, R.H. (1982). *In Search of Excellence*. New York: Harper Collins: 69.

27 *BusinessWeek*. (2006). "Everyone fears failure. But breakthroughs depend on it. The best companies embrace their mistakes and learn from them." July 10, 2006.

28 Nolen-Hoeksema, S. and Morrow, J. (1991). "A prospective study of depression and distress following natural disaster: The 1989 Loma Prieta earthquake." *Journal of Personality and Social Psychology*, 61: 105–121.

"LIFE IS A SERIES OF EXPERIENCES, EACH ONE OF WHICH MAKES US BIGGER, EVEN THOUGH IT IS HARD TO REALIZE THIS. FOR THE WORLD WAS BUILT TO DEVELOP CHARACTER, AND WE MUST LEARN THAT THE SETBACKS AND GRIEFS WHICH WE ENDURE HELP US IN OUR MARCHING ONWARD."

—HENRY FORD (1863–1947)

CHAPTER 7

REFLECTIONS ON "LEARNING FROM FAILURE"

A project failure can be a step toward subsequent success if we learn from our experience. Although many people have told us that we learn more from our failures than our successes, learning from failure is not automatic or instantaneous. We typically have a negative emotional reaction to a project failure. This negative emotional reaction interferes with the learning process. Learning from failure requires a process of managing emotions to maximize learning and personal growth.

Some project failures make us feel worse than others. Projects that satisfied our needs for competence, autonomy, and relatedness are more important to us and create a greater deficit in psychological well-being when they fail. The more important a project is to us, the worse we feel when it fails. These negative emotions consume information-processing capacity, which interferes with the learning process.

❂

Strategies for Managing Emotions to Learn from Failure

There are three approaches to managing these emotions, with the goal of maximizing our ability to learn from failure. The first is a *loss-oriented strategy* that focuses on building an understanding of why the project failed. As we develop a plausible story for the failure, we can break the emotional bonds to the project lost, which further enhances learning. However, this strategy has its costs. If we continuously focus on the project failure, our thoughts can turn to the emotions surrounding the event and lead to ruminations that can make us feel worse. This then begins to obstruct learning.

The second approach is a *restoration-oriented strategy* that involves both distracting ourselves from thinking about the project failure and addressing secondary causes of stress. Distraction minimizes the generation and intrusion of emotions. If we address and eliminate secondary causes of stress, the primary stressor (project failure) does not loom as large. However, this strategy also has its costs. It is difficult to suppress emotions that can lead to physical and psychological problems; these emotions will eventually resurface at perhaps an inopportune time. Also, the attention that is focused on distraction tasks is not allocated to the project failure, which is necessary to scan and process information for learning.

The third strategy is a combination of the other two. The *oscillation strategy* involves alternating the use of the other two strategies. This allows us to benefit from each while minimizing the costs of holding either one for an extended period of time. This process maximizes learning from failure by managing emotions. It helps focus attention on collecting information about why the project fails to construct a plausible account of the failure event. In doing so, we can break the emotional bonds to the project lost, reducing the strength of the emotional response and eventually eliminating it.

But when thoughts shift from the events leading up to the project failure to the emotions surrounding the event, we begin to feel worse, and this interferes with the learning process. It is then that a shift to a *restoration* orientation provides the opportunity to recharge our cognitive batteries. We regain information processing capacity that was previously engaged by emotions and begin to address secondary causes of stress. This can help reduce the overall negative impact of the project failure. When cognitive capacity returns, we can again focus on the project failure to further construct an account of the failure, break emotional bonds, and learn from the experience. Oscillation continues until our emotions no longer interfere with our normal (work) life and we have learned from the experience. This increases the likelihood that we will try again and not make the same mistakes. We have personally grown as a result of having experienced failure.

❋

When to "Pull the Plug" on a Failing Project to Maximize Personal Growth

Although emotions are triggered by project failure, a similar reaction is triggered when we realize that the performance of our project is terminal. It will fail; the only question is when. The length of this period of *anticipatory processing* influences how bad we feel when the failure event eventually occurs. Thus, it determines how strong an emotional reaction we will need to manage, to learn from failure and grow from the experience.

We sometimes have a choice of when to pull the plug on our projects.

We sometimes have a choice of when to pull the plug on our projects. Thus, the length of the period of anticipatory processing is within our control. Despite the economic rule of thumb telling us that we should kill the project as soon as we realize it will not provide acceptable returns, we know that most people do not follow this rule. Some people have argued that termination decisions that deviate from the economic rule of thumb are fundamentally flawed. Those people believe that our termination decisions are flawed because we are highly influenced by *sunk costs* (those we can never hope to recover) and/or we just don't want to have to admit our mistakes to ourselves and others. Some people may delay the decision to terminate a project as a *short-term coping technique*. The individual avoids the emotional pain by delaying the termination of the project, even though the long-term costs are increased as a result.

Deviations from the economic rule of thumb are not necessarily decision errors representing flawed thinking. If we think about success as occurring across a number of projects (not just one), we realize that personal growth is not just about minimizing financial costs but also about emotional recovery from failure. Although financial recovery is enhanced by immediately pulling the plug on the terminal project, emotional recovery can be enhanced by a moderate delay to allow the process of anticipatory processing to emotionally prepare us for the failure event. If this period is too short, we do not have time to prepare emotionally for the failure. When failure occurs, the negative response is great. If this period is too long, dealing with the terminal project is emotionally exhausting, reducing emotional reserves and increasing emotions when failure occurs.

The decision of when to pull the plug on a terminal project can enhance our personal growth (our ability to learn from failure and the motivation to try again) by optimizing this trade-off between the financial costs of delay and the emotional benefits of some delay.

❖

Emotions, Social Support, and Learning from Failure

Managing emotions and learning from failure are intimately intertwined. By managing loss orientation, restoration orientation, and the transition between the two, we can maximize the scanning for information about why the project failed and the interpretation of that information. As a result, we can learn from experience. However, some of us are more effective at this process than others. Those who are more emotionally intelligent are more aware of their own emotions and are better able to regulate these emotions. Such an ability helps employ more effectively the emotion-management strategies to make sense of the failure and personally grow from the experience. Furthermore, emotionally intelligent people can better recognize emotions in others and help them regulate those emotions. They are more capable of helping others deal with emotions generated by project failure.

> *Managing emotions and learning from failure are intimately intertwined.*

But it is not just individuals who can help regulate others' emotions; teams can have an *emotional capability*. Emotional capability means that the team has the norms and routines so that the team as a whole can manage emotions generated from the failure of a team project. More emotionally capable teams learn more from the failure and grow from the experience.

Emotionally intelligent individuals can enhance the team's emotional abilities to learn from failure and personally grow from the experience. Emotionally capable teams can enhance people's emotional intelligence and help them learn from experience. If we can build our emotional intelligence and the emotional capability of our team, we have improved our ability to learn from failure, and we can more effectively grow from the experience.

❁

Self-Compassion to Learn from Failure

The methods just discussed focus on a *cognitive strategy* (a strategy for guiding our thinking) for managing emotions to learn from failure. But an emotional approach also can enhance learning. This emotional approach helps us deactivate strategies that we normally use to cope with failure. That is, some people perceive failure as a threat to their self-esteem. Because they failed at this project, they see the failure as a signal that they are not a particularly worthy person. We don't like such feelings, so we activate ego-protective strategies such as downward comparisons and external attributions to dismiss the failure and defend our self-esteem. However, such strategies represent substantial obstacles to learning.

> *It is not easy to separate your mistakes from your overall evaluations of the self.*

Rather than perceiving failure as a threat to self-worth, a self-compassionate individual can separate the personal mistakes that led to the failure from overall evaluations of the self. This allows for a more thorough investigation and understanding of the negative aspects of yourself. It provides insights into the causes of failure. It is not easy to separate your mistakes from your overall evaluations of the self. It requires self-compassion—self-kindness, common humanity, and mindfulness. Individuals who can be self-compassionate when going through a hard time and feeling emotionally vulnerable are less likely to need the ego-protective strategies that both protect the ego and obstruct learning.

Individuals who are self-compassionate recognize that although their weaknesses and mistakes led to project failure, everyone has weaknesses and makes mistakes. Putting our actions in perspective with everyone else helps us tolerate our own flaws and inadequacies. This tolerance lessens the threat to the ego, deactivates ego-protective strategies, and frees the learning process from such obstacles.

Similarly, self-compassionate individuals can keep their emotions over project failure in balance with the opportunity to learn from experience. This distinction between the failure event and our self-worth allows us to approach feelings of emotions with curiosity and openness that enhance our ability to learn from failure. Self-compassion is an important emotion that you should develop to enhance learning from failure.

❂

Preparing for Learning from Multiple Failures

Throughout this book, I have emphasized the importance of approaching a project failure from the perspective that success is defined by how we do across all our projects, not just one. Therefore, it is important to deal with the emotions from a project failure in a way that achieves success with subsequent projects. Achieving success on subsequent projects requires you to learn from failure so that your likelihood of success is higher for the next project. You also must be motivated to apply this new knowledge to that project. There are two primary approaches to dealing with situations where we are likely to face multiple project failures.

The *normalizing failure* approach involves being desensitized to failure so that failure no longer generates a negative emotional reaction. This removes emotional interference to the learning process. However, this approach does not capitalize on the learning benefits provided by emotions—highlighting the importance of the project failure and focusing attention on understanding why it failed. This approach of eliminating negative emotion as an output of project failure has an unintended emotional consequence—a reduction in emotion as an input to projects. One such emotion is commitment, which is of critical importance for project success. Therefore, although normalizing failure might eliminate negative emotions, it may not enhance the likelihood of success on subsequent projects.

The second approach, *regulation*, is consistent with the philosophy of this book. With this approach, you do not want to eliminate emotion as an input or output. You want to manage it to enhance learning from failure and maintain, or increase, the motivation to try again. As you learn to cope with multiple project failures, you will be able to build your coping abilities. This belief in your ability to deal with the emotions triggered by project failure reduces anxiety in anticipation of the project failure. It also means that you will try harder and be more successful. You can build your coping ability. This can be enhanced through self-help support groups and by using rituals after project failures.

Concluding Remarks: Reflections and Advice to My Daughter

As I said in Chapter 1, "Managing Emotions to Learn from Failure," I was inspired to write this book by my father, who experienced the loss of our family business that he had created and managed for over twenty years. Recovery took a long time, but he made it eventually, and he learned a lot and personally grew from the experience. But this book is not for him; it is for the next generation. That is why a story from John Carroll on National Public Radio (NPR) caught my attention.[1] He recounted how, when sending his granddaughter off for her first day of kindergarten, he wished her success. But deep down, he wished that she would experience failure. Failure has power. It is from failure that she will learn. He reflected on his granddaughter's personality and that failures will make her feel bad. Of course he planned to comfort her, but he also would remind her of what she can do next time to avoid failure. He realized that a five-year-old is unlikely to understand that failure is a good thing, but he wanted her to understand that it is not the end of the world.

> *I want her to know that failure is not the opposite of success.*

My daughter is about to start kindergarten. After researching and writing this book, I wanted to reflect on what I had learned that could be passed on to my daughter as she starts this new phase in her young life. However, I am not lying when I wish her success. Success is a lot more fun than failure. But I want her to know that failure is not the opposite of success. Failure at specific projects occurs on the way to overall success—success in kindergarten, school, career, and life. The key is to learn and keep trying.

I realize that this is often easier said than done. Failure hurts. Sometimes you need to reflect on what caused the failure. Sometimes you need to give your mind a break and get on with other things in your life. Sometimes you need to recognize how you feel and manage these emotions. And sometimes you should look to family and friends for help in doing this.

Despite your mistakes, weaknesses, and failures, you are a good person—I care about you. I hope you realize that your failures are not an indication of how you should feel about yourself. Everyone fails at some time, and they feel bad when it happens. We are all in the same boat. Hold your emotions in one hand and all the information about the causes of the failure in the other. Look to your hand that holds the emotions to guide your search for making sense of the information that is in your other hand. But do not allow your emotions to become so heavy that it takes all your strength to keep your hand up. Keep the weight in both hands balanced.

As you go on newer and more exciting adventures, you will experience failure more often. These failures will still make you feel bad. But you will develop skills that will mean that you will not feel bad for long. You can learn from your failures. This will mean you will fail less often, or will allow you to take on even more exciting projects. I hope you go for the more exciting projects, confident that you have the downsides covered. If you do, I will have been a success!

❂

Endnotes

1   Jon Carroll. "Failure Is a Good Thing." *Morning Edition*, NPR, October 9, 2006.

INDEX

T-U-V

W-X

Y-Z

⚊⚊ Wharton School Publishing

In the face of accelerating turbulence and change, business leaders and policy makers need new ways of thinking to sustain performance and growth.

Wharton School Publishing offers a trusted source for stimulating ideas from thought leaders who provide new mental models to address changes in strategy, management, and finance. We seek out authors from diverse disciplines with a profound understanding of change and its implications. We offer books and tools that help executives respond to the challenge of change

Every book and management tool we publish meets quality standards set by The Wharton School of the University of Pennsylvania. Each title is reviewed by the Wharton School Publishing Editorial Board before being given Wharton's seal of approval. This ensures that Wharton publications are timely, relevant, important, conceptually sound or empirically based, and implementable.

To fit our readers' learning preferences, Wharton publications are available in multiple formats, including books, audio, and electronic.

To find out more about our books and management tools, visit us at whartonsp.com and Wharton's executive education site, exceed.wharton.upenn.edu.